A PORTION
IN PARADISE
And Other Jewish Folktales

THE B'NAI B'RITH JEWISH HERITAGE CLASSICS
Series Editors: DAVID PATTERSON · LILY EDELMAN

ALREADY PUBLISHED

THE MISHNAH *Edited by Eugene J. Lipman*
RASHI *Edited by Chaim Pearl*

IN PREPARATION

THE HOLY CITY *Edited by Avraham Holtz*
MAIMONIDES *Edited by Isadore Twersky*
THE PHILOSOPHY OF HERMANN COHEN *Edited by Eva Jospe*
BIBLE HISTORIES *Edited by Jonas Greenfield*
JUDAISM AND THE DEMOCRATIC IDEAL
    Edited by Milton R. Konvitz
THE BABYLONIAN TALMUD *Edited by Edward M. Gershfield*
THE KARAITES *Edited by Zvi Ankori*
MESSAGE OF THE PROPHETS *Edited by Shalom Paul*
Bahya Ibn Pakuda DUTIES OF THE HEART
    Edited by Alfred Ivry
JEWISH PIETY: JOSEPH KARO AND ELIEZER AZIKRI
    Edited by R. J. Zwi Werblowsky
EMANCIPATION READER *Edited by Alfred Friedlander*
JOSEPHUS *Edited by A. Wasserstein*
HOLOCAUST READER *Edited by Gerd Korman*
JUDEO-SPANISH LITERATURE *Edited by Moshe Lazar*
THE HASIDIC TALE *Edited by Joseph Dan*
JEWISH LAW *Edited by David Daube*

*Published in cooperation with the Commission
on Adult Jewish Education of B'nai B'rith.*

A PORTION
IN PARADISE

And Other Jewish Folktales

Translated by H. M. NAHMAD

W · W · NORTON & COMPANY · INC · NEW YORK

In memory of my father
Moses Nahmad
and my brother
Esra Nessim Nahmad

Contents

The Wisdom and Folly of Women   85

The Righteous and the Pious   107

Tales of Wit and Wisdom   129

The Golem   155

Acknowledgments

The growing interest in Jewish folklore during recent years demonstrates the need for a popular work devoted to this fascinating field. The present volume has been compiled with this interest in mind. In addition to the stories, legends and anecdotes which it contains, the introductory passages provide a background to the material. The editor would like to acknowledge his great debt to the many scholars, past and present, whose researches have facilitated the task of presenting to the reader *A Portion in Paradise*.

H. M. N.

Preface

The Nature of Jewish Legend and Folktale

Most of the stories in this volume are legends and folktales. What makes them Jewish is their cast of characters—the pious and the just, the martyrs and the sages, the scholars and the miracle-workers. They are set against a historical background reflecting the traditions of the Jews—their beliefs, customs, practices, and super-stitions. These tales also incorporate the lore of peoples among whom the Jews have sojourned during the long centuries of their dispersion.

Perhaps the most important characteristic of the Jewish folktale, distinguishing it from that of other peoples, is its strong ethical emphasis and content; its stress on the spiritual aspects of existence, on monotheism, piety, righteousness, and the performance of good deeds. The story and parable, and sometimes the animal fable, are used to point to a lesson or give moral instruction. The deeds of the just and the sage are held up as example and inspiration. To this same end, tales of the wicked, of tricksters, deceivers, liars, hypocrites, thieves and robbers, of the proud and the arrogant, also serve a purpose and point to a moral. The proud and the arro-

15

gant are humbled, the wicked meet their just desert, and the righteous are delivered from disaster. If the wicked man abandons his evil-doing, he is forgiven; a good deed or a charitable act can atone for sin.

Not all the characters of legend, of course, are wholly good or bad; many are ordinary human beings. Some are clever and quick-witted, others stupid, lazy, or ignorant. Humorous tales, usually of the anecdotal type, abound in Jewish story-telling. The humor may be wry or satirical. The ability to make one's fellows laugh and forget their trials and tribulations, even for a few brief moments, is accounted the greatest of virtues. Two sages walk in the crowded streets of the city arguing about who among men is the most deserving of Paradise. Even as they dispute, they come upon a crowd of people being entertained by a clown. Thereupon, one sage says to the other, "That clown is the man most worthy of a portion in the world-to-come."

Jewish legends also deal with miracles. Though this subject is by no means unique to Judaism, accounts and descriptions of miracles wrought in favor of the Jewish people, at crucial moments in its history, abound in Jewish literature. Miracles and miraculous happenings, the deeds of miracle-workers and wonder-rabbis are all part and parcel of Jewish legend. A principal performer of miracles is the prophet Elijah, and a favorite setting for marvelous happenings is the tomb of King David in Jerusalem.

Belief in demons and evil spirits became widespread during the post-Exilic period of Jewish history, following the Babylonian captivity. Jewish demonology is largely derived from ancient Persia and Babylonia, but whereas the demons are independent beings in Persian mythology, Jewish demons and spirits—of both sexes—are servants of the Almighty. They must submit to His will and are obliged to do His bidding. As in the case of other Jewish traditions and beliefs adapted from those of surrounding nations and peoples, the belief in the existence of demons and other supernatural beings is made to conform to the spirit of Judaism, to the idea of monotheism and the omnipotence of the Creator. The stories of demons and mischievous spirits eventually found their way into the folklore sections of the Talmud,* which contain many accounts of the goings-on of demons and kindred spirits in their relations with men.

Jewish demons go under a variety of names, such as *ruḥin, mazziqin, lilin,* each according to its kind. The *shedim* † are a popular and frequently encountered demon of Jewish folklore, and their chief is Asmodeus (or Ashmedai), known as the Prince of the Demons, who often appears in connection with stories about King Solomon. These demons propagate their kind like men, and their number is without limit. Like human beings, they eat and drink, make merry and die. They can assume at will many forms, human or not. Their abode is in trees, gardens, vineyards, caper ‡ bushes, ruined buildings, and desolate places.

The limitations of demons are described in the Talmud, in a story about some porters who were carrying a cask of wine and who sat down to rest. As they laid down their burden, a demon appeared and damaged their cask. The carriers then complained to the sage Mar bar Rab Ashi and sought compensation for the damage. The rabbi at once summoned the demon and placed it under a ban until a certain date when compensation was to be paid. The miscreant promised to pay but did not turn up until a few days after the fixed date. The demon explained his delay by telling the rabbi, "I had great difficulty in obtaining the money, as I was unable at first to find any that was without an owner." He then went on to explain that demons have neither the right nor the power to touch anything that is sealed, counted, measured, or tied up.

* The Talmud comprises the body of Jewish law and legend compiled in Palestine and Babylon during the early centuries of the Common Era. It embodies two elements: Halakhah and Aggadah. Halakhah (law) deals with legislation, legal discussions concerning civil and criminal law, interpretation of those laws, ceremonial, ritual and kindred subjects. *Aggadah* is an Aramaic word (in Hebrew, *Haggadah*) meaning *story, narrative, talk, homily*. It stands for the non-legal element—or folklore section—of the Talmud, the Midrashim or homiletic commentaries on the Scriptures and other rabbinical literature. These two elements are intermingled throughout the pages of the Talmud.
† Their Arabic equivalent is *jinn*.
‡ An aromatic shrub found in southern Europe and the Mediterranean countries.

Another Talmudic belief is that demons are said to abstain from intoxicating drink; hence the havoc they play in vineyards, and the damage to casks of wine. One rabbinic sage stated that evil spirits crowd the academies, stand by the side of brides, hide in crumbs fallen on the ground, in drinking water, in the diseases men contract, in oil in cooking vessels, and in the air. No mortal creature could survive if he actually saw their number, "for they are like the earth that is thrown up around a bed that is sown" (*Berakhot* 6a). The way to subjugate demons and render them powerless is to pronounce the Ineffable Name (of God). It is by this means that King Solomon was enabled to subdue Asmodeus and force him to carry out the royal commands.

Angels also have their place in popular Jewish tradition, and the most familiar in Jewish lore is the Angel of Death (in Hebrew, *Mal'akh ha-Mavet*). Stories about his encounters with mortals are numerous: he is the divine messenger who takes the soul from the body, and he appears among men in many different guises. In the Bible he is considered to be one of the host of "destroying angels." Because death is likely to be associated in Jewish tradition with sin, evil, and punishment ("charity saves from death"), and the Hereafter is expected to be free from death and evil, the Angel of Death is usually designated by pejorative terms such as Satan, the Tempter, the Accuser, the Adversary, the Evil Inclination.

Midrashic legends are filled with horrifying descriptions of the Angel of Death; there are tales of how the children of men use every stratagem to deceive the messenger and go out of their way to frustrate his designs. But in the end they have to answer to his summons, for it is as a divine command, even though it may be delayed for a time. Examples of this idea can be found in the two stories *The Prophet Elijah and the Angel of Death* (see page 33) and *King David and the Angel of Death* (see page 47).

In rabbinic literature the Angel of Death takes on greater independence. In a theological sense, he exercises a positive function in the divine scheme of things, and is considered one of the instruments of the Creator's will. Although Jewish legends have borrowed much from surrounding cultures, their three principal sources are, of course, the Bible, the Talmud and other rabbinic literature, and the great medieval collections. From Biblical sources we derive legends and stories inspired by the personalities and activities of the patriarchs and prophets; the Bible is the source of the legends of Elijah, David, Solomon, of the hero-tales, of miracles and wonders.

The Talmud, however, is the largest source of Jewish legend and folktale, anecdotes, parables, fables, fantasies, and tales of magic. There, rubbing shoulders, so to speak, with Israelite myths and legends, are examples of the legendary lore of Persia and Babylon, Greece and India. The Aggadah portions of the Talmud comprise a vast folk literature about Biblical heroes, sages, scholars, teachers, wise men, fools, angels, and demons. Many of the stories and tales, in anecdote and parable form, elucidate and interpret points of law, serving as illustrative examples. Some are of a moralizing and didactic nature, while others seem to be pure fantasy or what we would call "tall stories." The scholars and sages passed a portion of their time recounting fanciful tales to one another because, like all human beings, they loved to listen to a good story. Far from being dry-as-dust men immersed in their books of law, and aloof from the everyday life about them, they possessed a sense of humor; they loved good conversation and enjoyed battles of wit and the cut and thrust of debate. Yet underlying all this was the desire—and indeed, the duty—to educate as well as to amuse. These tales and anecdotes were told not only to entertain but, above all, to instruct and teach a moral lesson.

The medieval and post-medieval collections added substantially to the store of Jewish folk literature, though, strictly speaking, they cannot be classed as original source material. For the most part they are compilations of oral and older written tradition. They embrace elements from non-Jewish—both Christian and Islamic—as well as Jewish sources. Among the most famous of these collections is the *Ma'aseh-Buch* (Book of Stories), written in Judeo-German and published at the beginning of the seventeenth century. This book contains a wide range of tales, legends, and anecdotes, ranging from stories of the pious to folk tales culled from the peoples among whom the Jews lived. According to some authorities, the *Ma'aseh-Buch* was designed to take the place of non-Jewish collections which were extremely popular. Another well-known collection is the *Ma'asei Nissim* (Miracle Stories), which was particularly popular among the Jews of the Islamic countries of the Near and Middle East and the Mediterranean area.

In addition to these and other collected writings, there are the works of individual authors who traveled about listening to and setting down stories, tales, proverbs, maxims, and sayings they heard. They often made up stories. One such author is Joseph ben Meir ibn Zabara, a celebrated physician of Barcelona, Spain, who wrote and practiced his profession in the latter half of the twelfth century. Though a man of many talents and much learning, Ibn Zabara is known largely through one work, the *Sefer Sha'ashu'im* (*Book of Delight*), containing tales, scientific discussions, and proverbs. The recurring theme of some of the tales is the faithlessness of women.

From the Middle Ages onward in Eastern Europe a great crop of legendary tales grew up around pious and saintly men and the miracles and wonders they wrought. Chief among these figures were the Ḥasidim, a sect of pious Jewry which first made its appearance in eighteenth-century Eastern Europe.* Although these tales embrace a variety of ethical and religious themes and subjects, a great number of them could be described as wonder-tales —stories of the supernatural and the supernatural helper in time of need and distress, a favorite theme of Jews in that period. To this category belong the celebrated and well-known stories about the Golem and its famous creator, the learned Rabbi Judah Löw, the great rabbi of Prague (see pages 157–70).

What follows is a sampling of Jewish legends and tales from these various sources, reformulated and retranslated for this volume. Together, they reflect a number of facets of the Jewish vision of the world.

* A volume of Ḥasidic stories, edited by Professor Joseph Dan of The Hebrew University, is in preparation for this Jewish Heritage Classics Series.

Tales of
the Prophet Elijah

Introduction

The most popular and beloved Biblical figure in Jewish legend and tale is Elijah the Tishbite. Yet less is known about him than is known about all the other prophets of Israel. No book in the Bible bears his name, we have no writings attributed to him, and we know little of his family or origins. His designation, the Tishbite, may refer to a location in Gilead, the land east of the Jordan River.

In reality there are two Elijahs: the prophet, and the figure portrayed in Aggadic literature. The Elijah of Biblical narrative stands out as an upright, fearless, uncompromising figure, zealous in the pursuit of righteousness and the service of God. We see him as an outspoken critic of Jezebel (the wife of King Ahab), who introduced the worship of the Baal into Israel, and as the denouncer of Ahab for having caused the death of Naboth in order to take possession of the latter's vineyard. Elijah's encounter, in the name of God, with the priests of Baal on Mount Carmel (I Kings 18) is one of the dramatic highlights of his prophetic career. So zealous was Elijah that the Almighty had to administer a gentle rebuke to him in a vision (I Kings 19:13).

Throughout his life Elijah led a wandering existence, moving from place to place, frequently as a fugitive. On one occasion, forced to flee from the vengeance of Jezebel, he took refuge on Mount Horeb, where he rested and heard God's voice telling him to have patience. It was on that mountain that God manifested Himself, not by earthquake or fire or wind, but in the "still small voice" (I Kings 19:11–12). Elijah was fed by the ravens and sustained by a widow, for whom he performed miraculous deeds. He caused her barrel of meal and cruse of oil to last throughout three and a half years of famine, and when her son died the prophet restored him to life. Elijah departed his earthly life in a chariot of fire, borne by a whirlwind up to heaven. His last dramatic act was to fling down his mantle to be taken up by his faithful disciple Elisha (II Kings 2:13).

The other Elijah, the popular figure of Jewish tradition and the hero of rabbinic literature, bears a different character. This Elijah is bound by neither time nor space. He wanders over the face of the earth in many and varied guises, but usually as a Bedouin or Arab of the desert. He acts as a celestial messenger, a warner, and an adviser. He appears in times of distress and danger and befriends mystics and scholars. He brings consolation to the afflicted and chides the arrogant and the proud. Expectation and hope are associated with the prophet, for Elijah is regarded as the precursor of the Messiah. Malachi prophesies that God will send Elijah before the "advent of the great and dreadful day of the Lord" (Malachi 3:23). While the Bible describes Elijah's earthly life, rabbinical lore creates a "new" life for him, beginning with the transport of the prophet to heaven in a fiery chariot, and concluding only with the end of the human race and the appearance of the Messiah, son of David. In the Havdalah ceremony at the termination of the Sabbath, Elijah is associated with his traditional role as forerunner of the Messiah.

Two other attributes are associated with Elijah's name in Jewish ceremony and ritual: the Chair of Elijah and the Cup of Elijah. The Chair is used at the rite of circumcision (in Hebrew, *brit milah*), of which the prophet is thought to be the guardian spirit and witness. A special chair is customarily set aside for him during the ceremony. This custom is said to be based on Elijah's outcry: "for the Children of Israel have forsaken Your covenant" (I Kings 19:10), interpreted by the rabbis to mean that the Israelites had abandoned the rite of circumcision or the *brit*-covenant (Genesis 17:19). The Jews thus commemorate his zeal by regarding him as the patron of circumcision.

The Cup of Elijah is associated with the Passover Seder; the "fifth cup" (of wine) has given rise to popular belief in the invisible presence of Elijah. The linking of this custom with his name has its origin in a Talmudic dispute about whether four glasses of wine or five should be drunk during the Seder. The decision was left for the Tishbite to determine at the time of the Messiah. It is also said that an extra cup is to be filled for Elijah in case he should suddenly appear to announce the coming of the Messiah.

To the scholars and the pious with whom he came into contact, the Elijah of rabbinic tradition was particularly strict, and he would tolerate no backsliding on their part. He was always quick to show them where they had erred and to teach them hidden truths. Among the Talmudic rabbis with whom legend associates him most closely is Rabbi Joshua ben Levi. Once, during the Roman occupation of Palestine, the Romans threatened to destroy the town of Lydda unless a political fugitive, in hiding there, was surrendered to them. Rabbi Joshua, under this pressure, turned over the fugitive to the authorities. Elijah was so angry with him that he stopped his regular visits to the house of the sage for a long period.

One of the stories in the present collection (see page 35 ff.) describes a meeting between Rabbi Joshua and the prophet. Elijah teaches Joshua some of the "hidden truths" and shows him, as they journey from place to place, that all is not what it appears to the beholder. He counsels Joshua not to ask the "why and wherefore" of God's actions. In another version of this same tale, the first encounter of the two travelers is with a widow and not with a man and wife, as in the story given here. In addition to killing the widow's cow, Elijah kills her only son because, as he explains later to Rabbi Joshua, the boy would have grown up a murderer.

In the episode on page 33 ff., we find a version of a story describing the prophet's warning of a bridegroom against the coming of the Angel of Death. Another version, to be found in *The Book of Delight* by Joseph ben Meir ibn Zabara,* relates that a young man is given the liver of a fish washed up on the shore. A servant who has guided him on his travels to and from India tells him that if the liver is burned as incense in a house, no misfortune will enter. The young man marries a woman all of whose previous husbands have died immediately following the wedding ceremony. The bridegroom follows the advice of the servant and burns the fish's liver in the house, and lives. When he tries to reward the servant, the latter vanishes among the street crowds. The bridegroom's father, a man of piety, maintains that the servant was in fact the prophet Elijah in disguise, sent to deliver them from evil.

Muslim and Arab tradition has taken over many of the Jewish stories about Elijah as the worker of miracles and performer of wonders. In Arabic tradition Elijah is associated with the legendary figure of *al-Khidir* (Arabic for "the evergreen," indicating the popular belief that Elijah did not die as did other men). Another name is *Khidr Ilyas,* the "evergreen Elijah."

* Translated by Moses Hadas, New York, Columbia Paperback, Columbia University Press, 1960.

A Portion in Paradise

Numerous are the tales of poor scholars whose study of the Law was hindered by their extreme poverty. One such student was Rabbi bar Abuha. One day he met the prophet Elijah and complained bitterly that his poverty was so great and his cares so burdensome that he had no time to study Torah.

"Come with me," Elijah said, and led Bar Abuha straight to paradise. He instructed the scholar to spread his cloak on the ground and gather up the leaves growing on the trees there, which he would be able to sell on earth for a high price. The rabbi followed Elijah's advice and was about to depart with his load when a heavenly voice called out, saying: "So the good Rabbi bar Abuha already anticipates his portion in the world-to-come by taking it during his earthly life."

When the rabbi heard these words, he hurriedly emptied his cloak of the celestial leaves he had gathered. On his return to the temporal world he was able to sell his cloak for a large sum of money because of its wonderful fragrance, acquired from the leaves of paradise. That money enabled him to live free from worry and care and to devote himself to the study of the Torah.

Another legend centers on Rabbi Ḥanina ben Dosa, the famous teacher of Mishnah who lived eighteen hundred years ago. He too was very poor and was forced to cast about for some means of relieving his poverty. His wife urged him to ask for some of the reward due him in the hereafter. One day a golden leg from his table in paradise came down to him. But Ḥanina's wife, repenting of her earlier advice to her husband, feared that the table in paradise might become unsteady with one leg missing, so she urged him to pray that it be returned. This he did, and the table-leg was taken back to its rightful place.

In another version of this tale,* a certain well-to-do merchant, though Godfearing and observant of his duties, began to develop an unholy lust for gold. He took to praying that he might stumble upon some hidden treasure. On his journeys back and forth to his warehouse or to the house of prayer, he used to keep his eyes on the ground in the hope that he might find something of value.

One morning, while he was in his counting-house writing out his accounts, an old man of gaunt appearance, wearing a shabby Bedouin cloak, appeared in his doorway. He greeted the merchant: "Peace be with you, my master."

"What do you want?" the merchant asked the old man.

"I want nothing," was the reply. "I've come with good tidings. Your prayers have been answered. Before the day is out you will find riches." Then the old stranger vanished as suddenly as he had appeared. That evening, on his way home, the merchant came upon a chair-leg made of gold. He picked it up quickly and looked around to make sure nobody was watching. Trembling with excitement, he took it back to his warehouse and hid it. He could hardly eat his evening meal for thinking of his discovery. Noticing his preoccupation, his wife asked if anything was the matter, but he told her nothing. That night he could hardly sleep for thinking of how best to profit from the gold chair-leg.

But next day his efforts to dispose of the treasure met with no success. Those to whom he showed it were suspicious that the merchant had stolen it. Eventually he took it to a goldsmith of his acquaintance, a shrewd and honest man. The goldsmith examined it

* Heard by the author of the present collection in his boyhood.

and shook his head, saying: "My friend, I cannot do anything for you. Were I to sell all my property at a profit I could not purchase even a tenth of this piece of gold. Only kings and princes possess gold chairs, and what would they want with a single leg?"

The gold chair-leg that nobody wanted became a burden, and the merchant began to regret having found it. He went to sleep and dreamed that he stood on the threshold of paradise. There he was met by an old man who introduced himself as the prophet Elijah. The merchant at once recognized him as the same old man who had visited him in his warehouse.

"Come with me," said Elijah, "and I'll show you the seat you will occupy in paradise among the elect." He led the merchant through the celestial sphere until they came to a great table made of gold, around which were many chairs, also made of gold. The prophet pointed to one. "That's the chair you will occupy in the hereafter," he said. And the merchant saw that it had only three legs.

"But how can I sit on a chair that has only three legs?" asked the bewildered merchant. "And why is it so?"

"Because one leg has already been given you while you are still on earth," was the reply. The merchant woke from his dream trembling with fear. All that day he prayed that the gold chair-leg be taken back. That night he had another dream. He stood again at the gates of paradise, and on the threshold there again was the prophet Elijah. He beckoned the merchant to follow him. When they reached the great table, the merchant saw that his chair had four legs like all the other chairs, and he rejoiced. In the morning he awoke refreshed and in good spirits, and after reciting the morning prayer and breaking his fast, he hurried to his warehouse and the place where he had hidden the gold chair-leg the day before. But it was no longer there. When he went out later into the market place, he caught sight of an old man in a tattered Bedouin garment moving among the crowd. The merchant hastened to intercept him, but the prophet Elijah vanished before he reached the spot.

The Seven Years of Blessing

It once happened that a rich man lost all his wealth and property and was compelled to hire himself out as a laborer in order to support his wife and children. One day, while the man was laboring in the fields, the prophet Elijah appeared before him disguised as a wandering Arab and said: "Peace be with you, my friend. It has been decreed that you shall enjoy seven years of wealth, happiness, and comfort. Tell me, do you want these years of plenty now, or later, during the seven closing years of your existence?"

Taking his interlocutor for a magician or sorcerer, the laborer told him to go on his way, as he had nothing to give him for his sorcery. The disguised Elijah went on his way but returned three times more and each time asked the man the same question.

"I want nothing from you," said the prophet. "Just tell me when you want the seven good years granted to you." The man said that before he could reply he would have to ask his wife. Elijah said he would be back the following day for the answer. Meanwhile, the man went to his wife, told her of his encounter with the stranger, and asked what she thought he ought to do.

"Tell the stranger," said the wife at once, "to send us the good years now, for surely the near is preferable to what is far off."

When Elijah came the following day and asked for a decision, the man, mindful of his wife's advice, replied: "Let the seven good years come to us now."

"It shall be as you ask," said Elijah. "Leave your labors and go home. Even before you reach your house, the Lord will have blessed you and granted you good fortune."

The poor man went home at once and found that the Tishbite's prophecy had come true. His children had been digging in the ground and had found a great treasure. The man was overjoyed and gave thanks to God for His bounty and praised his wife for her good advice. Said that good woman: "Since we are certain of God's mercy for seven whole years, let us practice charity and feed the hungry and succor those in distress, so that perchance God may continue His grace toward us at the end of the seven years and grant us further prosperity to the end of our days."

So the two of them, husband and wife, went about doing good and practicing charity toward the needy. And no person in distress appealed in vain to them. Whatever they dispensed in the way of help to the poor and needy, the woman wrote down in a book. The seven years passed, and again the prophet appeared before the man.

"The time has come," Elijah declared, "when you must return the gift I granted you."

"My lord," said the man, "when I accepted your gift I did so with the advice and consent of my wife. Let me now, I beg of you, consult her once more and tell her of your request before I return the gift you bestowed upon us." Elijah gave him permission to do what he asked, and the man went to his wife and told her that the stranger had come to take back what he had given them seven years earlier.

"Go to our benefactor," said the good woman, "and tell him that if he has found anyone more faithful than we, who will guard better the treasure and use it for good, then we shall return the pledge entrusted to us."

And God hearkened to the words of the pious wife, for He saw that she and her husband had used the riches entrusted to them for good and that they had performed many good deeds. So He continued to bestow His mercy upon them and allowed them to keep the wealth granted them through Elijah the prophet to the end of their days.

The Prophet Elijah and the Angel of Death

A story is told of a man of wealth and piety who had a daughter of great beauty and intelligence. But she had had the misfortune of having lost three husbands in succession; on each occasion, after the wedding ceremony, the bridegroom had died. Because of these experiences, the girl had vowed that she would never marry again.

One day a poor kinsman, her father's nephew, who lived in a distant town, came to their house to seek help from his rich uncle. As soon as he set eyes on the daughter, he asked for her hand in marriage. His uncle tried to dissuade him by acquainting him with the fate of his predecessors, but to no avail, for the young man was determined to marry the girl, come what might. Finally, after much argument, the father agreed to the marriage, and in due course the wedding took place.

While the bridegroom was standing under the wedding canopy, the prophet Elijah appeared to him in the guise of an old man and said: "I want to give you some good advice, my son. When you are seated at the wedding feast, a beggar in dirty ragged clothes and with matted hair and unpleasant countenance will approach you. As soon as you catch sight of him, rise and invite him to sit beside you; give him food and drink and be prepared to grant any request he may make of you. Do as I tell you, and you will be protected against all harm." And with these words of advice Elijah vanished.

As the guests sat down to the wedding-feast, a stranger appeared at the door exactly as Elijah had prophesied. He wore a dirty, tattered garment, and his hair was long and matted. The bridegroom followed Elijah's advice and treated the beggar hospitably. After the feast, the beggar revealed himself as the Angel of Death sent to take the soul of the bridegroom. All the supplications and protests of the bridegroom failed to move the messenger; he refused to grant him a single day's respite. The most that he granted was permission for the bridegroom to bid farewell to his wife and family.

When the bride saw what was about to happen, she approached the Angel of Death and engaged in a disputation with him. She said: "The Torah exempts the newlywed from all duties for a whole year. For is it not written that he who marries a young wife is exempt from military and other duties and is to remain at home for a whole year so that they may both enjoy conjugal bliss? If you deprive my husband of his life you will give the lie to the Torah."

Confronted with this argument, the Angel of Death sought guidance from the Almighty. Thereupon God commanded him to annul the decree of death against the bridegroom. Thus when the kinsmen of the young man came to mourn his death, they remained instead to rejoice and praise the Lord for the lease of life granted him.

Rabbi Joshua ben Levi and the Prophet Elijah

It is related that the pious Rabbi Joshua often prayed to God to grant him a glimpse of the prophet Elijah. One day the Almighty answered the rabbi's prayers, and Elijah appeared before him. "Is there anything you want of me?" asked the prophet. "Say it and I shall fulfill it."

"Yes, my lord," replied Rabbi Joshua. "Let me be your companion on your wanderings so that I may witness your deeds and your wonders among men, and so learn knowledge and wisdom from you."

The prophet thought over this request, and said: "You would not be able to understand all that you see, and you would ask me the reason for every action and every deed I perform, and it would be a burden to me to answer your questions."

The rabbi replied, "I promise I will not inquire concerning your actions or weary you with my questions. I beseech you only to let me accompany you on your journey." So Elijah allowed Rabbi Joshua to go with him, on the condition that his companion should not question him concerning any miracles and wonders and signs he might perform. Should the rabbi disobey the prophet's injunctions, they would have to part company at once.

The two then went forth and journeyed in silence until they

came to the house of a poor and needy man who possessed nothing in this world save one cow. When the man and his wife saw the two wayfarers, they greeted them and bade them welcome. They put a humble meal before their guests and invited them to pass the night beneath their roof. When morning came, the prophet and the rabbi arose and prepared to continue their journey. Before doing so, however, Elijah prayed for the destruction of the cow, and the animal died. Then they went on their way. The good Rabbi Joshua was puzzled by this deed. Greatly troubled and forgetting his promise, he asked Elijah why he had caused the death of the poor man's cow after being shown honor and hospitality by its owner.

"Remember the condition I made," replied the prophet, "that you would ask no question or inquire after the reason for my acts and deeds. I will answer your question if you are prepared to part company from me." Thereupon Rabbi Joshua, fearing that he would be banished by the prophet, held his peace.

They continued on their way and toward nightfall came to the house of a certain rich and miserly man. They entered but were offered neither meat nor drink. They stayed the whole night without food, and no generosity was shown them. In the morning, Elijah noticed that one of the walls of the house was in a ruined state, and the rich man expressed his wish to rebuild it. The prophet prayed, and the wall was miraculously built up. Rabbi Joshua was greatly surprised when he saw what Elijah had done, but, mindful of the Tishbite's warning, he kept silent.

The two travelers set out once more and in the evening came to a great synagogue. The building was adorned with silver and gold, and every man was seated in accordance with his rank and dignity in the community. When the congregants saw the two strangers, they began to argue among themselves whether or not to offer them food and lodging. One said, "Who will feed and lodge these poor wayfarers?" Another replied, "They are in no need; for have they not brought bread and water and salt with them?" In the end nobody extended hospitality, and the travelers had to pass the

night in the synagogue with only bread and water to sustain them.
In the morning the two arose and, before setting forth, Elijah addressed the men of that place, saying: "May the Almighty make
you all leaders and head men of the community." After which the
two companions departed.

As they journeyed on, the pious rabbi became increasingly exercised over the strange actions of his companion; but he kept his
counsel and said nothing. At sundown they arrived at a town
where they were received with honor and rejoicing by the inhabitants and were lodged in the finest house in the town. Food and
drink were set before the two tired men, and they passed the night
in comfort. In the morning Elijah prayed for the people. "May it
be God's will," he prayed, "that only one man among you be made
head of your community."

On hearing these words, Rabbi Joshua could no longer contain
his curiosity. "I pray you, my lord," he cried, "tell me now the reason for your strange behavior."

The prophet replied, "Since it appears that you are resolved to
part from me, I shall acquaint you with the meaning behind my actions. Concerning the poor man's cow which I caused to die, I did
what I did because I knew that it had been decreed that his wife
should die that very day. I prayed to the Almighty to accept the
cow, the couple's only possession, as a ransom for the wife. They
showed kindness to the stranger, and good fortune will soon be
theirs. As to the rich man whose fallen wall I rebuilt, I know that
beneath the wall's foundation is a cache of treasure. Had I let that
miserable man build the wall himself, he would have discovered
the treasure. And what of the mean-hearted men for whom I
prayed and asked that they should all be leaders and chiefs? This I
did because it will turn out ill for them. Where there are many
chiefs, dissension and division reign, their counsels are brought to
naught, and their place is destroyed. I prayed for the righteous of
the town, who received us hospitably, and asked that only one
among them become their chief. In that way they will derive bene-
fit, for there will be neither dissension nor division in their coun-

sels, and their affairs will be directed properly. As the proverb has it, 'The ship that has more than one captain sinks.' "

As Elijah was about to leave, he turned to the rabbi and said, "Before I depart from here, let me give you counsel that will profit you. If you see the wicked prosper, do not be troubled, for their prosperity and fortune will in the end be their downfall. Should you see the righteous and the just afflicted with misfortune and in need and distress, and without possessions and riches, do not be grieved in spirit or rise in anger. Do not ask the Almighty, with doubt in your mind and heart, why this is so. Know that He is just and merciful and that He sees the ways of all men. Do not say, 'Lord, why have You done this?' "

With these parting words, Elijah bade farewell to Rabbi Joshua, the son of Levi, and was gone.

Tales of David
and Solomon

Introduction

LET NOT THE WISE MAN GLORY IN HIS WIS-
DOM, NEITHER LET THE MIGHTY GLORY IN HIS
MIGHT.

—JEREMIAH 9:22

As there are two Elijahs, so there are also two Solomons. The one is the King Solomon of the Biblical account, an historical figure, and the other is the Solomon of myth and legend in rabbinic and other literatures. While Elijah is ascetic and hermit-like, Solomon is pictured as a worldly-wise hedonist.

The name of Solomon, King of Israel, son of David the servant of God, is synonymous with wisdom and perception and the power of judgment. On the basis of accounts given in I Kings and because the authorship of the Book of Proverbs is attributed to him, a vast lore has been built up around his name and person. We read that God appears at night in a dream before Solomon at Gibeon, and asks him what he most desires. Solomon answers that he wants wisdom and understanding to enable him to distinguish between right and wrong and help him judge the Children of Israel. Solomon's wisdom becomes a byword among the nations, and kings and princes travel from far and near to hear his words and listen to his judgments (I Kings 5:9–14).

Solomon revealed his powers of judgment and his wisdom early in his reign, when he settled the case of the two harlots who both laid claim to the same child. The two women lived in one house and had each borne a child within the same hour. During the night one of the babies had died, and its mother had gone to her companion's bed while the latter was asleep and exchanged her dead child for the live one. In the morning, when the deception was discovered, the mother of the living child put her case to Solomon and claimed the child; the other woman made the same claim. After hearing both stories King Solomon ordered the child to be cut in two with a sword, with each woman taking a half. The real mother begged the king to let the other woman have the child rather than slay it. Thus Solomon knew which of the two women was the real mother. "And all Israel feared the king for they saw that the wisdom of God was in him to do judgment" (I Kings 3:16–18).

This simple exercise in knowledge of human psychology became the basis of many similar stories in both Jewish and non-Jewish lore to illustrate the judgment of Solomon. This kind of tale has always been popular in the East, among the Islamic peoples, and a complete Solomonic lore has been created, based to a large extent on Jewish sources but drawn from other traditions as well.

The glory of Solomon, the great Temple he built in Jerusalem, his magnificent palaces, his wives and concubines, his stables, his power and dominion over neighboring kings and princes—these are but a few of the elements making up the vast store of myths, legends, and tales around the king's person. We are told that he held sway over demons and other supernatural beings as well as over the elements and over every creature that crept on the earth or flew in the air. With the aid of his ring, on which was inscribed the Ineffable Name, he could bend all to his will. Even Asmodeus, Prince of the Demons, was not immune and was forced to assist, as were other demons, in the construction of the Temple. Of the story of Solomon's meeting with the Queen of Sheba there are many versions, similar in substance, but differing somewhat in detail, mainly in the questions and riddles put to Solomon by the queen.

Despite Solomon's glory, his power and wisdom, Jewish tradition never allows us to forget that he was a human being with human failings and weaknesses. He incurred the wrath of God for his arrogance and pride, his vast harem, his material possessions and his introduction of pagan practices into the royal court.

Many stories have as their theme the reminder to King Solomon of his mortality. In the fable on page 71 ff., Solomon is admonished for his pride by the queen of the ants.

A number of tales about Solomon's wisdom and power of judgment in his youth link him with his father, David. In these episodes it is the young Solomon who delivers final judgment, not his father; indeed, David here seems to act only as a foil to his son and successor. In "Enmity between Man and Serpent" (page 51 ff.), the litigant is not satisfied with the verdict of David, and in the end it is Solomon who delivers judgment. In "The Value of a Boiled Egg" (page 44 ff.), it is again Solomon who decides the case in a matter of compensation in which his father has failed. The latter type of story is common in the folk literature of many Eastern peoples; there is a Persian version of the same story, dealing with the value of a hen instead of an egg.

The Value of a Boiled Egg

One day the young men who served David the king were eating a meal of boiled eggs. One of these lads, being very hungry, devoured his eggs quickly. Faced with his empty plate, he asked his neighbor to lend him one of his boiled eggs.

"Certainly," said the second youth, "if you will promise me before witnesses that when I ask you for repayment you will return the egg to me with the full amount it would have earned for me during the time elapsing between now and then." The borrower of the egg agreed and promised before all present to fulfill the conditions.

After a time had passed, the lender asked the borrower to repay him. "Yes, by all means," replied the latter. "You lent me an egg and I shall repay you with another egg." But the lender asked in addition for a large sum of money which he claimed the egg would have earned him during the elapsed time. A dispute ensued, and the two went to King David and put their case before him. On arriving at the gates of the royal palace, the two young men met the king's son, Solomon, whose task it was to ask all litigants what their business was with his father. They acquainted Solomon with their case, whereupon he said: "Take your case to my father, then let me know what judgment he has given."

The two youths went before the king, and the lender of the boiled egg produced his witnesses, who testified to the original bargain. The lender claimed from the borrower the amount the egg would have yielded during the time that had elapsed since the bargain had been made. After listening to plaintiff and defendant, King David ruled that the borrower had to pay his debt in full.

"But, Sire," pleaded the borrower, "I do not know how much the debt is."

Questioned by the king, the lender explained: "In the course of a year, the egg would have produced a chicken," he said. "The following year that chicken would have given birth to eighteen more chickens; and in the third year every one of those eighteen would have given birth to another eighteen, and so on. Therefore, I demand a large sum of money from the borrower—the value of the hundreds of chickens that I would have sold at a profit."

After hearing the king's judgment, the borrower of the egg was in a distressed state of mind. As they left the palace Solomon again appeared at the gates. The borrower told him that King David had decreed that he would now have to pay a large sum of money as the equivalent of the amount the egg would have earned.

"Listen to me," said Solomon to the youth, "and I will give you some sound advice. Go out into the fields and station yourself beside a ploughed field. Every day companies of the king's troops pass there. When you see them approaching take a handful of boiled beans and throw them on the ground. If the soldiers ask you what you are doing, say: 'I am sowing boiled beans.' And when they laugh and ask: 'Whoever heard of boiled beans yielding crops?,' say to them: 'And whoever heard of a boiled egg producing a chicken?' "

The youth did as Solomon advised. When the soldiers asked him what he was doing, he replied that he was sowing boiled beans. "Whoever heard of anything boiled taking root and yielding fruit?" they asked in amazement. "And whoever heard of a boiled egg bringing forth a chicken?" was the quick retort.

Every company of troops that passed asked the same question

and received the same answer. News of the young man's strange behavior reached the ears of King David, who summoned him into the royal presence. "Who advised you in this matter?" asked the monarch.

"It was my own idea," the young man replied.

"I think not," said the king. "I see the hand of my son Solomon in it." At this, the youth confessed that it was in truth Solomon who had advised him to act in this manner. David then summoned Solomon and asked him to pronounce judgment in his stead.

"This lad cannot be held responsible for something that cannot be said to exist. An egg boiled in hot water can never be hatched, and thus cannot be considered as a potential chicken."

King David had to admit the rightness of his son's judgment, and commanded the youth to pay to his companion the price of an egg, and nothing more.

King David and the Angel of Death

King David once prayed to God to inform him of the measure
of his days (Psalms 39:5), to tell him when his end on earth was
to come. His prayer was not granted, for God has decreed that no
man shall know the hour of his death. David then begged God to
inform him of the day of the week on which he would meet his
end, and it was revealed that it would be on the Sabbath. David
wanted his death postponed so that he could be permitted to die
the Sunday following, but God would not grant his request. "For,"
said He, "the reign of your son Solomon will begin on the Satur-
day of your death, and no reign may overlap by a hairsbreadth the
time assigned to the reign of another." David thereupon asked
God to allow him to die on Friday, the day before. But again his
request was denied; the Almighty said that He delighted more in
one day passed by David in the study of the Torah than in a thousand burnt-offerings brought by his son Solomon in the Temple.

Now it is known that the Angel of Death has no power over a
man who is occupied with the study of Torah. So David spent
every Sabbath day in the study of Torah without respite, thus hop-
ing to outwit the Angel of Death. When David's appointed hour
arrived, the Angel of Death appeared in order to take the king's
soul. But he was powerless to do anything, since David did not in-

terrupt his study of God's Law for a single instant. The messenger, tired of waiting, decided on a ruse that would enable him to carry out his mission. One Sabbath, which also happened to be the first day of Pentecost, the Angel of Death entered the garden behind the royal palace and made a loud noise. Hearing it, David left his studies and went down to the garden by way of some steps to ascertain the cause of the disturbance. One of the steps gave way and David fell down and was immediately killed. As it was the Sabbath, the king's body could not be removed from the spot; but neither could it be left all day in the hot sun. Solomon, his son, who had command over all the birds, summoned the eagles to cast their shadows over the dead king and stand guard over him.

Where the Kings of Judah Sleep Their Last Sleep

It happened one day that a wall in the city of Jerusalem fell in and was in need of reconstruction. The governor ordered the wall to be rebuilt with stones from the old city wall, and a number of strong young laborers were hired to carry out the task. Among them were two friends who, one morning, turned up late for their work. On being taken to task by the foreman, they promised they would go on working while their fellow laborers were resting. This they did, and they continued to remove stones from the city wall. They had just removed an unusually large stone when they discovered an opening leading to a cave.

"Let's go down," said one of them, "and explore the cave. Perhaps we may be lucky and find some hidden treasure."

They descended and walked along an underground passage until they reached a vault, where they found themselves in a large hall with marble pillars decorated with gold and silver. In a corner of the chamber the two laborers saw a sarcophagus on which rested a scepter and crown of gold. To the left of the sarcophagus stood another tomb, and farther along the hall were more tombs. The two friends, their curiosity whetted, were about to explore further when a violent gust of wind suddenly hurled them to the ground. There the two lay until the evening, when they were brought back to con-

49

sciousness by a loud voice calling: "Arise and get you away from this place."

Frightened, the two men quickly rose to their feet and hastened from the underground hall. They appeared before the governor of Jerusalem and related what had befallen them. Now it happened that there lived in the Holy City a pious man called Abraham, and the governor summoned him at once. He asked the old man if he knew anything about the tombs in the vault.

"Yes, my lord," replied Abraham. "There is a tradition among our community that the tombs of King David and King Solomon, and the tombs of the other kings of Judah, are situated in that subterranean vault."

The following day the governor sent for the two laborers so that he could send them to the cave again, but such had been their shock that they were too ill to go. They sent a message to the governor saying that it was evident that it was not the will of the Almighty that any man should again visit the chamber of the tombs. The governor thereupon ordered that the cave's entry be walled up so that no person could ever again discover the place where the kings of Judah were sleeping their eternal sleep.

Enmity Between Man and Serpent

One very cold day, an old man was walking in a field when he found a snake lying motionless. He raised his stick to kill it, but the reptile made no movement. The old man took a closer look and saw that it was frozen with cold. Taking pity, he picked the snake up and put it in his bosom in order to warm it. Before long the snake recovered and began to wind itself around the old man's body until he was in danger of being crushed to death. He protested and asked the snake why it was crushing the life out of him when he had saved it from dying of the cold. In reply the snake said that Holy Writ commands it, saying: "You shall bruise the heel of man."

The old man said they should both go to a court of law so that their case could be judged. The snake asked who would be the judge between them. "Whomever we meet first on the road," was the reply. The snake agreed and eased its pressure on the man.

On the way they met an ox, whom the old man stopped and told what had happened. After listening to his story the ox turned and asked what the snake had to say.

"I'm only doing what is right, for in our Torah it is written that there shall be enmity between man and serpent," said the serpent.

The ox signified his agreement with the snake, and said to the old man: "The snake is right. Though you do it a kind deed, it will do you an evil one in return. It is the way of the world to repay good with evil." With this judgment the ox went on its way. But the old man was not satisfied. A little later they met an ass. The old man stopped, told his story, and asked the ass to judge fairly between him and the snake. The donkey then asked the snake to plead its case, and the same answer was given the ass that had been given the ox. After hearing man and reptile, the ass delivered its judgment.

"The snake is surely right in repaying good with evil and a good turn with a bad one, for that is its nature and the way creatures behave in the world." And with these words the ass too went on its way.

The old man was still not pleased and, with the snake still coiled round him, made his way to Jerusalem to put his case before King David. But the king could not help him. In despair, the old man left the royal presence. Passing a pit, he saw Solomon, the wise son of King David. Solomon's stick, set with precious stones, had just fallen into the pit, and his attendants were trying to recover it, but in vain. Then Solomon in his wisdom ordered the men to dig a waterway round the pit and fill it to the brim. The stick then floated to the surface and was easily reached. When the old man saw this, he said to himself: "Perhaps this young man can deliver me from the snake." So he approached Solomon and acquainted him with the whole story.

"Did you take your case before my father for judgment?" asked Solomon.

"I came before your father, the king, but he told me that he could not help me," replied the old man.

Solomon thereupon took the old man back to the palace, and they stood before King David. Solomon asked his father why he did not give judgment against the snake. The king answered: "Because I judged according to what is written in the Torah." But Solomon was not satisfied and asked to be allowed to judge between the man and the snake. The king agreed, and Solomon asked the snake why it had treated the old man in such a manner, and what it wanted of him. "I want to kill him," was the snake's reply, "because Holy Writ commands it, saying: 'You shall bruise the heel of man.' "

Solomon then said: "First free the man from your grip and descend to the ground, for it is written that neither party to a lawsuit shall enjoy an advantage over the other. Both of you must stand." The snake, thereupon, did as commanded and uncoiled itself from the man. Solomon repeated his question and received the same answer. He then turned to the old man and said: "God's command to you was to bruise the head of the serpent." The old man raised his stick and smote the head of the snake, killing it.

The Pasha's Sword

Many stories are told, particularly among the Sephardim, about the tomb of David in Jerusalem and the miracles and marvels connected with it. One well-known legend concerns the pasha's sword.

The pasha, it is related, was standing one day in front of David's tomb and looking through the aperture in the mausoleum. Somehow he let his sword fall so that it dropped into the cave where the tomb was. Since the sword was of great value, ornamented and encrusted with precious stones, the pasha was anxious to recover it. A Muslim was lowered by a rope through the opening to retrieve the sword, but when he was drawn up out of the tomb, he was dead. Another man was let down in his place and met with the same fate, as did a third and a fourth after him. But the pasha was determined to get back his sword, even if every man in Jerusalem were to perish in the attempt.

Finally, a *qadi* (Muslim judge) suggested a way to recover the sword.

"My lord," he said to the pasha, "rather than sacrifice the lives of the faithful in this manner, would it not be better to send for the Hakham-Bashi (Chief Rabbi) and command him to send one of his flock to be lowered into the tomb to get back my lord's sword? King David—peace be upon him!—is an Israelite, and he will surely not harm one of the sons of Israel!"

The pasha acted on the *qadi*'s advice and sent a messenger to the house of the Hakham-Bashi, with the threat that should the rabbi refuse to send one of his community to bring up the sword, all the Jews of Jerusalem would suffer.

The Hakham was in a dilemma. If he obeyed the pasha's order, he would be desecrating King David's tomb; if he refused, his people would be in danger. For three days he and the community fasted and prayed at the grave of Rachel the matriarch. On the fourth day the Hakham decided to cast lots to choose the man to undertake the task. The person chosen was the beadle of the synagogue. He prayed and purified himself, and prepared to descend into the royal tomb. He was lowered by a rope through the aperture. After a while the bystanders heard a weak, barely audible voice calling from the depths: "Draw me up!"

The people pulled on the rope and drew up the beadle, pale and trembling, grasping the pasha's sword in his hand. At the sight of him, all present prostrated themselves and cried: "Blessed be the Lord God of Israel!" And the Jews of Jerusalem rejoiced greatly.

The beadle handed the sword to the pasha but refused to reveal what he had seen in the tomb. Later, however, he told the Hakham-Bashi that on entering the royal tomb he had seen a great light; then an old man of commanding appearance had stood before him and handed him the sword.

King Solomon and the Queen of Sheba

When King Solomon was in cheerful mood and good spirit by reason of wine, which, it is said, gladdens the heart of man, he used to invite to his palace the princes and rulers of neighboring lands and divert them with all manner of entertainment. He regaled them with song and dance, and the court musicians played on their instruments. Solomon was master over the beasts of the fields and the birds of the air, the denizens of the forests and the creeping reptiles, the spirits and the specters, the *shedim* and the *jinn,* and was able to summon them all so that he could impress his guests with his power and might. On such occasions he would order the royal scribes to call the beasts and the birds and the spirits by name, and they all assembled of their own accord, neither bound nor fettered nor guided by human hand.

It once happened that the hoopoe was missing from the assembly of birds and was nowhere to be found. This angered King Solomon greatly, and he commanded his servants to find the hoopoe and chastise it severely. When the hoopoe finally appeared of its own volition, Solomon asked why it had tarried and where it had been when the rest of its fellows were summoned.

The hoopoe bowed low before the king and, wishing him many long years of glory, said, "Hearken to my words, O king of the world, and receive them with favor. Three months have passed since I took counsel with myself and resolved upon a certain action. I have eaten no food, and no water have I drunk, in order that I might fly across the entire world to find a country or nation in all the universe that does not acknowledge my lord as king. One day as I was flying, I passed over a country whose capital is Kitor in the East. It is a wonderful city, the likes of which I have never before seen. The dust in that city is more valuable than gold, and there is silver in the mud of its streets. The trees in that land are from the beginning of Creation and they are nourished by the waters of the Garden of Eden. The men of Kitor wear crowns on their heads. The people do not know war, nor are they skilled in the use of bow and arrow. Their ruler is a woman whom they call the Queen of Sheba. If it please my lord the king, I shall gird my loins in the manner of a hero and fly to this city of Kitor in the land of Sheba. I shall bind its princes in chains and fetter its governors with bands of iron and bring them before my lord."

Thus spoke the hoopoe. Its words pleased King Solomon, and he at once summoned the scribes of the royal court. They wrote a letter and tied it to the hoopoe's wing. The bird uttered its accustomed cry and rose into the sky attended by a company of birds, and they flew to the city of Kitor in the land of Sheba, where a woman ruled. At the very instant that they descended in the morning light, it happened that the Queen of Sheba had just left her palace to prostrate herself before the sun, which she worshiped. Suddenly a great darkness came over the city as the mighty concourse of birds blocked the sun's light. The queen raised her hand, rent her garment, and trembled with fear. When the hoopoe alighted at her feet, she saw the letter tied to its wing. She untied it and read the letter, which said:

"From Solomon, King of Israel, greetings and peace to you and your nobles. Know you that the Lord God—blessed be His Name! —has appointed me master over the beasts of the field, the birds of the air, the demons and the spirits. All the kings of the East and the West and the North and the South come to greet me and pay homage to me. If you will come and do likewise, I shall honor you above all the princes and rulers who attend me. Should you refuse to come and render me homage, I shall surely send kings and legions and riders against you and your kingdom. You will ask who are these kings, these legions and riders of King Solomon, and I shall answer that the beasts of the fields are my kings, the birds of the air my riders, and the demons and spirits my legions. The demons will throttle you in your beds at night as you sleep; the beasts will slay you in your fields; and the birds of the air will feed off your flesh."

On reading these words, the Queen of Sheba once more rent her garments. She called her elders and counselors and princes before her. "Do you not know what King Solomon has written to me?" she asked them.

"We do not know this King Solomon, nor do we recognize him, and we hold his kingdom as nothing," they replied. But the queen was not reassured by their answer, nor did she place any trust in their words. Instead, she commanded that all the ships of her country be assembled and loaded with costly gifts, fine woods, pearls, and precious stones. With these she sent to King Solomon six thousand youths and maidens born in the same month of the same year, on the same day and at the same hour. They were all of equal size and stature, and all were clad in garments of purple. With them they took a letter from their queen to King Solomon, in which she wrote: "From the city of Kitor to the land of Israel is a journey of seven years; but as it is your wish that I visit you, I shall hasten on my journey and be in Jerusalem at the end of three years."

When the appointed time drew near, Solomon sent Benaiah, the son of Yehoyada, to meet her. Now Benaiah was a man of surpassing beauty, of whom it was said that he was the evening star that outshines all the other stars, that he was like a rose that grows by a brook. When the Queen of Sheba beheld him she descended from her chariot. When Benaiah asked why she had come down, she replied: "Are you not King Solomon?"

"No," answered Benaiah, "I am only one of his servants attending him and standing in his presence." Thereupon the queen turned to her princes and nobles and cried: "If you have not beheld the lion, you have seen his lair; if you have not seen King Solomon, you have beheld the beauty of him who stands in his presence."

Benaiah then took the Queen of Sheba into the presence of the King of Israel. Now Solomon had heard that the queen had hairs on her feet, and in order to find out the truth of this he had devised a scheme. He had built a floor of crystal over a pool which the Queen of Sheba would have to cross in order to reach him. She was deceived by this trick, and as she approached him she raised her garment in order to prevent its getting wet, and in doing so she bared her legs. The king noticed hair on her bare feet and said to her: "Your beauty is the beauty of a woman, but your hair is the hair of a man. Hair is an adornment to a man, but to a woman it is a blemish."

In order to test Solomon's wisdom, the Queen of Sheba put a number of riddles to him. "If you can solve these riddles," she said, "I will know that you are indeed wiser than all men; if you cannot, I will know that you are as other mortals." *

She then put the following question to him: "Who is he that was not born nor has died?"

"The Lord of the universe, blessed be His Name!" replied Solomon.

The queen then asked: "What is it that never moves when it is living, but moves only after it has been killed?"

"A ship," was the answer. "It is made of the wood of living trees that have been cut down."

"Now tell me, my lord the king, who were the three who ate and drank on earth but who were not born of male and female?"

"The three angels who visited Abraham."

The Queen of Sheba then ordered that the sawn trunk of a

---

* Many versions of the riddles asked by the Queen of Sheba are to be found in both Jewish and Islamic traditions.

cedar tree be brought. She asked Solomon to tell her which end had been the root and which end the branches. Solomon had the trunk cast into the water, and one end sank while the other end floated on the surface. "The end that sank was the root, and the part that floated on the surface was the end where the branches were," answered the king.

The queen then prepared another test for Solomon's wisdom. She summoned the boys and the girls of the same size and age and wearing the same purple garments, and said:

"Distinguish between the males and the females."

Solomon signalled to his eunuchs and they brought nuts and roasted ears of corn to distribute to the whole group. The boys, lacking the modesty of the girls, received them in their laps, lifting up their dresses,* while the girls put the nuts and corn in the veils which served them as head coverings. Solomon then turned to the queen and said: "Those are the boys, and these the girls."

The Queen of Sheba put to Solomon many more riddles, and every one he solved, upon which the queen exclaimed in wonderment: "You indeed surpass all other men in wisdom. Blessed be your God."

* Males usually wore skirt-like garments.

King Solomon and Asmodeus

During the building of the Temple of the Lord, King Solomon pressed into service not only the finest craftsmen and masons among men, but also the supernatural beings over whom he had been granted command, the demons, the devils, the *shedim, jinn,* and others of their kind. Chief among these was Asmodeus (or Ashmedai), Prince of the Demons, who is described as cunning, malignant, and having immense strength and power. Although his nature is to do harm to the children of men, he is able, and indeed often ready and willing, to perform acts of kindness. Asmodeus can foretell the future and render himself invisible at will. But at the same time he can be made to serve man by the use of the Ineffable Name, and be compelled to do what is bidden by those who pronounce the Name. Thus King Solomon, by the power of his signet ring (said to have been given him by the Archangel Michael in a dream), upon which was engraved the Ineffable Name, was able to gain power over Asmodeus and compel him to carry out his commands. How the King of Israel first met the Prince of the Demons is told in the following story.

King Solomon was about to build the Temple. And the stone for its building was to be dressed before being carried to the holy site

(I Kings 6:7). The stone for the building of the altar, however, was not to be fashioned by tools of iron, for that is forbidden by the Torah (Exodus 20:22). In his dilemma over how to fashion the stone for the altar, Solomon consulted the rabbis. "How can I accomplish this task without using tools of iron?" he asked them.

Now one of the rabbis recalled that there existed an insect which possessed the power of cutting through stone and the hardest substances. "This insect is called the *shamir*," he said. "With this insect Moses once cut the precious stones of the Ephod" (Leviticus 8:7).

"And where may this *shamir* be found?" asked the king. To which the rabbi replied: "Conjure up a male and a female demon and ask them the whereabouts of the *shamir*. Perhaps they know where this insect can be found and will reveal it to you." The king did as the rabbi and his companions suggested, and conjured up two demons, one male and one female. They appeared before the king but refused to reveal the secret, whereupon Solomon ordered them to be tortured. But in vain, for the two demons declared that since they did not know the dwelling-place of the *shamir,* they could not reveal it to the king. In the end they suggested that perhaps Asmodeus, Prince of the Demons, could tell the king where the *shamir* was to be found. Solomon then asked the demons where he could find Asmodeus.

"Asmodeus lives on a high mountain," they answered. "There he has dug a great pit which he uses as a cistern in which to store water for his use. Now, every morning before ascending to heaven in order to study there in the school of wisdom and hear the decrees of the Assembly on High, he covers the cistern over with a stone of great size and seals it with his seal. Every day after his return from his heavenly visit he examines the seal carefully. After satisfying himself that the stone has not been tampered with, he removes it, drinks his fill of the water, replaces the great slab over the water-cistern, then seals it again and takes his departure."

King Solomon then decided to find out if the demons were speaking the truth. So he sent for his faithful servant and counselor, Benaiah ben Yehoyada, and charged him to capture the Prince of the Demons. Before setting out on his mission, Benaiah obtained a magic chain and a ring upon which was engraved the Ineffable Name. He also took skins of wine and some wool. When he arrived at the mountain dwelling of Asmodeus, Benaiah went to work. First he made a hole in one side of the cistern to drain off the water and plugged it with some of the wool he had brought. He then made another hole higher up, into which he poured the contents of the wine skins, and he plugged that too. Benaiah then hid behind a nearby tree to await the return of Asmodeus.

Soon Benaiah was conscious of a disturbance in the atmosphere, and in a short while he saw Asmodeus descending from heaven. Asmodeus examined the seal carefully and, seeing that no one had interfered with it, he lifted the stone slab. To his surprise he found the cistern filled with wine instead of the water he had left there. Since Asmodeus, like all other demons, regarded wine as an abomination and abstained from drinking it, he shrank from touching it, repeating to himself: "Wine is a mocker, strong drink is riotous; and whosoever reels because of it is not wise" (Proverbs 20:1). In the end, however, his thirst proved too strong to resist, and he drank until his thirst was quenched. Overcome by the wine's effects, Asmodeus lay down and soon fell into a drunken sleep. Benaiah emerged from his hiding-place and fastened round the neck of the sleeping demon the magic chain he had brought. When Asmodeus awoke to find himself fettered, he fell into a rage and let out a mighty roar. He tried to break the chain, but Benaiah called out in a loud voice: "The Name of the Lord is upon you!" Whereupon Asmodeus ceased his struggles, knowing they were of no avail. Benaiah then set off on the return journey, leading the now-powerless Asmodeus as captive.

On their way back to Jerusalem, a number of strange things happened. They passed a palm tree, and Asmodeus rubbed himself against it, whereupon it became uprooted and fell to the ground. A little farther along they came upon the humble hut of a poor widow who, on seeing them, pleaded with the demon not to rub himself against it lest it fall down. Asmodeus complied with the woman's plea and bent back rather quickly. In doing so, he broke a bone in his body, whereupon he said: "This is what is written: 'And a gentle answer breaks the bone.' " Continuing on their way, they came upon a blind man who had strayed from his path. At once the demon prince took the man's arm and set him on his way. A little farther on they met a drunkard who had lost his way, and Asmodeus directed him aright. Shortly after this encounter, a wedding party passed them on the road, making merry and rejoicing, at the sight of which Asmodeus wept. The travelers continued on their way until they came to a shoemaker's booth. There they heard a man ordering a pair of shoes to last him seven years. At this, Asmodeus burst into loud laughter. And when he saw a magician at his tricks, the demon jeered and scoffed at him.

At last they arrived in the Holy City and at the royal palace. There Benaiah told King Solomon about the strange behavior of Asmodeus on the journey. After being made to wait three days, Asmodeus was admitted to the king's presence. Solomon then asked the demon to explain his actions on the journey. In reply, Asmodeus said:

"I guided the blind man on his way because I had heard it said in heaven that he was one of the righteous and would inherit the world-to-come, and that whosoever did him a service would earn a portion in the hereafter. As to the drunken man who had lost his way, I set him aright because I had heard in heaven that although he was wicked, he had once done a charitable act. I wept at the sight of the wedding party because I knew that the bridegroom was destined to die within thirty days, and that his widow would have to wait thirteen years for her husband's brother who is still an infant (Deuteronomy 25:5–10). And how could I do other than laugh when I heard a man ordering a pair of shoes to last him seven years, when he was not sure of living even seven days? The magician merited my scorn because he was sitting on a vast treasure buried in the soil beneath him, yet did not know it; at the same time he was pretending he could foretell the future and solve mysteries."

Having thus spoken, Asmodeus took a stick and measured off four cubits on the floor before Solomon. "When you die," he said, addressing the king, "you will be buried, and you will possess in all this world no more than four cubits of earth. Although you have conquered the world, you are still not content and must needs vanquish me too and make me captive."

Said Solomon: "I have made you my prisoner because I wish to build the Temple. Since it is forbidden to use tools of iron in fashioning the stone for the altar, I must have the *shamir* to split the stone, and I have had you brought here against your will so that you may reveal to me the place where the *shamir* is to be found."

"I do not possess the *shamir*," Asmodeus told the king, "nor has it been committed to my charge. The *shamir* was put in the charge of the Angel of the Sea, who in turn entrusted it to the moorhen. The bird has sworn an oath to return it to the Angel of the Sea."

The king of Israel marveled at what the prince of the demons had told him, and asked what the moorhen had done with the *shamir*.

"The moorhen," answered Asmodeus, "carries the *shamir* to a bleak rocky mountain which she cleaves asunder by means of this miraculous insect. As you know, there is no substance, however hard, that can resist the *shamir*'s power. Into the cleft so made, the moorhen carries fresh grass, herbs, and seeds of plants. When the valley is covered with all manner of vegetation it becomes a place fit for habitation."

Thereupon Solomon sent Benaiah and many servants to search out the moorhen's nest. He ordered Benaiah to take a globe of glass with him. When at last they found the nest, they saw that it contained a young brood. So Benaiah covered the nest with the glass globe, and they all awaited the return of the mother bird. When the moorhen came back and saw her young, but was unable to reach them because of the glass, she went to fetch the *shamir* so that it might split the globe. At that very moment, however, as the moorhen was about to put the insect to the glass, Benaiah gave a great shout. He so startled the moorhen that in her fright she dropped the *shamir*. Benaiah snatched it up and took it back to Jerusalem, where it was used in the building of the Temple. And King Solomon kept Asmodeus with him until the House of the Lord was completed.

Solomon and the Four Winds

One day King Solomon was sitting in his chamber dispensing justice when his young son Absalom appeared in a state of agitation. On being asked the cause of his excitement, Absalom replied, "As I was returning to the palace I came across a poor widow sitting by the wayside holding an empty wooden bowl and weeping bitterly. Scattered on the ground around her was spilled flour. When I saw her distress I advised her to come before you and put her complaint to you against the evil-doer who had robbed her of her flour. She will come soon, and I ask you, my father, to let me seek the guilty person and mete out punishment to him in accordance with our Holy Law."

Solomon rose from his throne and set his son in his place. He clothed the youth in his royal robes, placed the crown on his head, and the scepter of power in his hand. But the ring which gave him dominion over the winds and the spirits Solomon kept on his finger. In a short while the widow appeared in the audience chamber. As she was about to acquaint the king with her misfortune, Absalom raised his hand and motioned her to be silent.

"Since I know of the evil that has been done you, tell me only the name of the guilty person and I shall have him punished forthwith."

Making obeisance to both father and son, the widow said:

"As I was returning home with the flour I had just bought to bake bread for the Sabbath, a great gust of wind blew up, snatched at my bowl, and scattered the flour all over the road. I wept because I have no more money to buy new flour with which to make bread for my Sabbath meal."

Absalom looked toward his father for guidance. Whereupon Solomon kissed the blue stone in his ring and summoned the first of the four winds of heaven. There was a noise like the beating of mighty wings, and the West Wind entered the chamber through the open windows. Its head was covered with green hair and the feathers of its wings were moist with sea spray. The West Wind prostrated itself before the Lord of the Ring. When Absalom asked the wind to give an account, the wind addressed Solomon:

"While flying over the Isle of Cyprus I saw naked men digging to extract the green metal out of the rocks. I saw them smelting the ore and drawing the copper from it to clothe the roof of the Temple which you, Sire, are building on Mount Zion for the glory of God. But as for this woman, I neither saw her nor touched her property."

Solomon listened to the West Wind's account and, with a gesture, dismissed it from his presence. Again kissing the blue stone in his ring, he summoned the second of the winds—the East Wind. There was a noise like the beating of mighty wings, and the East Wind entered the audience hall through the open windows. Its head was covered with red hair and its wings were yellow from the sands of the desert. It prostrated itself before Solomon and, ignoring the angry accusation of Absalom, addressed the king:

"I came from the hot deserts and rested awhile over the mountains of Lebanon. There I observed men laboring in the deep forests cutting down cedar trees a thousand years old. The laborers were fashioning great beams from the trees to support the roof of the Temple which you are building on Mount Zion for the service and glory of God. As for this woman, I neither saw her nor laid hand on her property."

With a motion of his hand, Solomon dismissed the East Wind, then kissed the blue stone on his ring and summoned the third of the winds—the North Wind. There was a noise like the beating of mighty wings, and the North Wind blew in through the open windows. Its head was crowned with white hair, and its huge wings were white like the winter snows. It prostrated itself before the king. Absalom demanded that the North Wind confess its guilt, but the wind turned to Solomon and said:

"I flew over the marble quarries of Lydia and blew cooling air into the faces of the men who were quarrying the stone from the mountains. I saw them cut the marble into blocks and polish them and prepare them to serve as cornerstones for the Temple which you, Solomon, are raising on Mount Zion to the glory and service of God. As for this woman, I neither saw her nor touched her property."

Solomon thereupon dismissed the North Wind, and, kissing once more the blue stone in his ring, summoned the fourth of the winds —the South Wind. There was a noise like the beating of mighty wings, and the South Wind flew into the hall through the windows. Brown hair grew on its head and its wings were red like the coral in the southern seas. The South Wind alighted in front of the Lord of the Ring and bowed low before him. Absalom looked at the South Wind with anger in his face and shouted: "Since your brother winds are innocent of the crime against this poor widow you must be the culprit. Admit your guilt!"

"Indeed, it is true. I am guilty of the crime," replied the South Wind.

At these words, Absalom, filled with righteous anger, raised the scepter to smite the South Wind, but his father restrained him and bade the South Wind speak.

"My lord the king," began the South Wind, "I was flying high above the shore of Arabia, and the seas below me were calm and clear, when suddenly I heard loud cries of distress. Looking down, I espied a ship from Egypt sailing toward the coast of Arabia with some three hundred men, women, and children aboard. They were peasants and their families, driven from their land by famine and drought to seek fresh pastures in the oases of Arabia. I saw that their vessel had sprung a leak and was about to sink. The sailors tried to steer it toward the shore, but the water was already washing over it, and the ship was still some distance from dry land. It looked as if all those aboard would perish within very sight of land. I was greatly moved by their plight, so I descended and spread myself upon the surface of the water and blew with might and main against the waves, and against the sails of the sinking ship so that it raced toward the shore, enabling its passengers to land in safety. At the very moment, the tip of my wing happened to touch the widow's bowl of flour, overturning it."

When the South Wind had finished its tale, a deep silence descended on the hall, and no word was spoken. Then Solomon dismissed the South Wind from his presence and commanded his treasurer to give the widow a hundred gold pieces, and sent the woman away in peace. Absalom, silent and abashed, took off his father's robe and crown, surrendered the scepter of power, and came down from the throne.

Solomon and His Pride

Solomon, mighty king of Israel, was never allowed to forget that he was a mortal like other mortals, subject to the divine law and God's commandments, and that one day he would go the way of all earthly beings. Many stories are told of how this truth was brought home to him.

Now Solomon possessed a great carpet woven of green silk and embroidered with many fanciful images and designs. It is said to have measured sixty miles in width and sixty miles in breadth. It was used to carry the king and his entourage, his ministers, the wild beasts, the birds, and the demons attendant on him through the air from one country to another. One day, when the son of David had been boasting of his prowess and his wisdom, they happened to fly over the country of the ants. As they did so, Solomon heard the voice of an ant saying to its fellow ants: "Go and hide yourselves lest the armies of the mighty King Solomon crush you." These words angered Solomon, who commanded the wind to bring the carpet to earth. He summoned the ant which had spoken, and asked why it had spoken out in that way:

"I am the queen of the ants," the ant replied.

"Why did you say to your subjects, 'Go and hide yourselves lest the armies of the mighty King Solomon crush you'?" asked Solomon.

"Because I was afraid they might interrupt their praise of God in order to gaze upon you and your armies, and thus bring down the divine wrath upon their heads and be destroyed."

"And now," said Solomon, "I wish to ask you a question."

"Then take me in your hand," demanded the queen of the ants, "for it is not good that the asker of questions be high while the one being questioned be low."

So Solomon took the ant up into his hand and held her before his face. "Now ask your question," she said.

"Is there anyone in all the world greater than I?" the king asked.

"Yes," replied the queen ant. "I am greater than you."

"How so?" asked the king.

"Because," replied the insect, "were I not greater than you, God would not have led you to me to place me in your hand."

At these words Solomon's anger was kindled, and he threw the ant to the ground. "Do you not know who I am?" he shouted. "I am Solomon, son of David, peace be upon him."

But the ant was not impressed. She admonished the king and reminded him of his earthly origins. Solomon put the ant down and went away humbled. He returned to the carpet and commanded the wind to rise and bear him and his entourage aloft. As the wind lifted up the carpet, the queen of the ants cried after Solomon: "Go in peace; but remember the Name of the Lord and do not aggrandize yourself!"

The wind bore the carpet higher and higher until it cleft the air between heaven and earth. After a while, King Solomon espied below a magnificent palace built of gold. At his command the wind abated, and the carpet descended gently to earth. Taking with him as attendant Asaf ben Berekhya, the prince of the sons of men, and the prince of the demons, the king walked round and round the palace seeking a gate through which to enter; but he found neither gate nor door. After further search, the chief of the demons came upon an eagle who was seven hundred years old. The great bird blessed the name of the Lord and greeted Solomon. The king asked the eagle if he knew of any door by which they might enter the palace.

"No, my lord," replied the king of birds, "I do not know; but I have a brother nine hundred years old who may be able to answer your question." Solomon had the eagle's brother brought before him, but he, too, was unable to answer. He suggested that his elder brother, who was thirteen hundred years old and possessed of greater knowledge than the two younger eagles, be consulted. So the eldest of the brothers was conducted into Solomon's presence. By reason of his great age, this eagle, unable to fly, had to be carried on the wings of the younger birds. He blessed the name of the Lord and saluted the king, who then repeated his question.

"By your life, my lord, I know not," was the reply. "But my father—peace be upon him!—once told me that there was a gate on the west side of the palace which had been covered over by the dust of the ages and could not be seen."

Solomon thanked the aged eagle and commanded the wind to blow away the dust. It did so, and a great iron gate was revealed. Attached was a lock on which were inscribed the following words:

"Know, O men, that we the dwellers in the palace lived therein for many years. When famine came upon this place we used pearls instead of wheat to grind into flour, but to no avail. When we were about to die, we bequeathed the palace to the eagles."

Another inscription told them where the keys to the different chambers of the palace were to be found. Solomon followed the directions written down, and with the keys opened door after door of the palace, whose apartments were made of pearls and precious stones and silver and gold. He wandered through the wonderful building until he came to a great hall of precious stones which had three doors.

On the first door was written: "Son of man; let not time and fortune deceive you; for you, too, must waste and wither away and in the end depart from your place and rest beneath the earth."

On the second door was inscribed: "Do not hasten, but go slowly and take heed, for the world is taken from one and given to another."

On the third door were these words: "Take provision for the journey and furnish yourself with food while the day is yet light; for you will not dwell on earth forever, nor will you know the day of your death."

In one of the rooms Solomon saw a number of statues and idols, of which one looked like a living person. As the king drew near, it cried out in a loud voice: "Arise, you sons of Satan, for Solomon has come to destroy you!"

Suddenly a tremendous noise and confusion filled the apartment, and the statues came alive and shouted and bellowed until the earth quaked and the sound of thunder filled the ears. Whereupon Solomon pronounced the Ineffable Name, and the tumult subsided and there was silence. The statues were overthrown and the Satans fled and cast themselves into the sea out of fear of Solomon, son of David.

Then Solomon went up to the lifelike image and drew from its mouth a silver tablet on which was writing that Solomon could not decipher. As he was pondering the matter, a youth from the desert appeared at his side. "Give the silver tablet to me, my lord," said the young man, "and I will interpret the words for you. They are in the Greek tongue." Solomon gave him the tablet and the youth read out to him these words:

"I, Shaddad, son of Ad, ruled over a hundred thousand provinces, and rode a hundred thousand horses, and had a hundred thousand kings under me. I slew a hundred thousand horses and warriors, but when the Angel of Death came to me I was powerless against him."

And Solomon, King of Israel, wondered greatly at these words, and left that place meditating upon the transience of all earthly power and glory.

The Game of Chess

It is related that King Solomon invented the game of chess and so naturally surpassed all others in playing it. One day he was playing with Benaiah ben Yehoyada, his faithful servant and counselor, who realized he was about to lose to Solomon. As he was pondering his next move on the board, there was a disturbance outside the palace, and the king rose from his place to see what it was. Quickly, Benaiah removed one of the king's pieces. A minute or two later, Solomon returned to the game and resumed his playing but failed to notice what had happened. Without the missing piece he was unable to overcome his opponent and so lost the game. Solomon concealed his anger at being defeated in a game over which he was master, but said nothing.

After Benaiah had departed, King Solomon set up the chessboard again, reconstructed the game, and replayed it by himself. By this means he discovered the trick played on him while he was away from the board. He thought how best he could punish Benaiah for his trickery and resolved in his mind that one day he would make his servant confess his wrong in public. In the meantime, however, Solomon continued to play with Benaiah—always defeating him in the end—without once mentioning his companion's single triumph.

Now it happened one evening that Solomon perceived two fur-
tive-looking men, carrying empty sacks, loitering outside the palace. The king guessed from their appearance and demeanor that
they were thieves. Quickly he changed out of his royal garments
and put on the clothes of a palace servant and went out to the two
men.

"Peace be with you, brothers," he greeted them, "I see that you
and I are fellows of the same craft; I also am skilled in your calling. Follow my advice and we shall all profit. I have the keys to all
the rooms of the palace where the king's treasures are stored. At
midnight when all are asleep I'll open up the rooms; we will take
what we can of the treasure and share it equally among the three
of us."

When midnight came, the disguised king opened one of the
treasure rooms, and as the thieves were filling their sacks Solomon
roused the palace servants and the guard, and the robbers were
seized and thrown into a dungeon for the night. The following
morning the king went to the Sanhedrin, which was presided over
by Benaiah ben Yehoyada. Solomon had a question to put before
the learned members of the court. What punishment, he asked,
should be meted out to a thief who had robbed the king? When
Benaiah heard this question he was seized by fear and trembling.
Seeing no criminals before the court, he imagined that the king in
his wisdom was pointing the finger of accusation at him. For, he
reasoned within himself, to whom else could the king be referring?
Had he not robbed the king of victory recently, while his back was
turned? Benaiah, certain that he was about to be punished for his
misdeed, prostrated himself before Solomon, begging his pardon
and forgiveness.

"My lord the king," he cried, "I am in truth the thief of whom
you speak. When we were playing chess together, I removed one
of your pieces while your back was turned so that I might win the
game."

When the king heard the confession, he was pleased that Benaiah had acknowledged his trick. He bade his counselor arise and

assured him that he harbored no malice against him. He told him that, when he had put his question to the Sanhedrin, he had had in mind real thieves who had tried to steal the royal treasure during the night. And in such manner did Solomon carry out his vow that he would compel Benaiah to confess in public how he had beaten the king at chess by a trick.

Adares, King of Arabia

Solomon's mastery over the demons and spirits once enabled him to come to the aid of Adares, king of Arabia. Adares one day sent a message to the king of Israel asking him to save his country —Arabia—from a powerful demon who, in the form of a wild wind, blew over the country from dawn to dusk. "So terrible is its force," wrote the Arabian king, "that neither man nor beast can prevail against it." He begged Solomon to send someone powerful enough to capture this tyrannous demon, and promised in return that he and all his people would serve King Solomon and that the land of Arabia would live in peace with Israel.

Solomon thereupon summoned one of his faithful servants and commanded him to take a camel and a leather flask and go to Arabia, where the evil wind was blowing. The servant also received the king's signet ring.

"When you reach Arabia and the place where the evil spirit is blowing so fiercely," said the king, "place the signet ring in front of the mouth of the leather flask, and raise them both toward this evil wind. Once the flask is inflated, tie up its mouth quickly, for the demon wind will be inside. Then seal the flask securely with the ring, place it on the camel, and return. If, on the way, the demon offers you gold and silver and riches to set him at liberty, do not heed his request, but inquire from him the places where gold and silver are hidden. Now go, and God go with you, and bring back the demon from Arabia."

After arriving at a certain spot in Arabia, the servant waited for the dawn when the demon wind would begin blowing. When dawn came, the servant placed the leather flask on the ground and held the ring in its mouth, so that the wind blew through the ring and into the flask, causing it to swell. Once the flask was inflated, the man knew the demon was safely inside. He quickly tied the mouth of the flask, the while pronouncing the Name of the Lord. He then sealed it securely with the signet ring, as his master Solomon had commanded.

Since the demon was now sealed within the leather flask, the terrible wind ceased blowing over the land. The Arabians rejoiced greatly and praised the Almighty, who had endowed Solomon, son of David, with such wisdom and power. They sent the servant of King Solomon home with gifts and honor. On his arrival in Jerusalem the servant placed in the Temple the leather flask holding the demon of Arabia.

The building of the Temple was almost complete, save for the great cornerstone on its pinnacle. Neither workmen nor demons had so far been able to raise the stone. As Solomon was thinking over the matter, the leather flask containing the Arabian demon suddenly rose and, approaching the king, abased itself before him. Solomon commanded the demon in the bottle to stand up. "Who are you and what is your calling?" he asked. "I am the demon able to move mountains and overthrow them," was the reply.

"Can you then raise this stone and lay it in its place?" asked King Solomon.

"Yes," answered the demon, "I can do so; and with the help of the demons who rule over the Red Sea I can raise a pillar of air and support this stone."

Solomon thereupon commanded the demon to flatten itself and the leather flask to appear as if emptied of air. Solomon then placed it under the heavy stone, and the demon was thus able to set the stone in its appointed place. Then the demon who rules over the Red Sea appeared and raised up a column of air, and the column remained suspended in mid-air supporting the stone.

When King Solomon asked who this demon was and what was his business, the demon replied that he had once sat in the first heaven, being the descendant of an archangel. He had fought the other spirits in heaven and hardened the heart of Pharaoh against Moses. He had incited Pharaoh and the Egyptian hosts to pursue the Children of Israel through the Red Sea. When the Israelites had passed safely through the waters of the Red Sea, the demon had remained in the sea and its waves had overwhelmed the Egyptians. And when Solomon heard this account, he wondered greatly and gave praise to Almighty God.

The Three Litigants

Three merchants who were partners often traveled together on business. One of their journeys happened to fall on a Friday, the eve of Sabbath; and as they were unwilling to carry any money on their persons on the Sabbath, they decided to hide their gold and silver in an agreed place until sundown the following day. This they did and went to rest. At midnight one of the three companions arose and, going to the hiding place, removed the money and put it in another place. Then he returned to where his two partners were still asleep.

On the following day, after the Sabbath, the three men went to the spot where they had concealed the money, but of course it was gone. They accused one another of having stolen the money, arguing that, since no one else knew where the money was hidden, it could only have been removed by one of them. After much heated argument, they finally agreed to submit their case to King Solomon. The king heard their story and bade them return the next day, when he would give his verdict.

After the three disputants had departed, Solomon reflected for a while on the matter. Finally, he decided to employ a stratagem. He would make the thief confess out of his own mouth to his crime. The next day, the three merchants appeared before Solomon at the appointed hour to receive his judgment. The king then spoke.

"Before judging your case," he said, "I would like to have your opinion on a difficult matter, for I have heard that you are clever merchants and shrewd men of affairs accustomed to dealing with all manner of people. There once lived in a certain town a youth and a girl who loved each other. They both swore an oath never to marry anybody else without first obtaining each other's consent. One day the girl's parents, according to custom, betrothed their daughter to another man, but she refused to become his wife until she had fulfilled her promise to the youth and had sought his consent. She told the man to whom she was betrothed about the oath she had sworn. 'Then let's go to this youth,' he said, 'and ask him to free you.' So, taking with them a large sum in gold and silver, they went to the young man's house to offer him the money if he would free the young woman from her pledge. 'I have been faithful to my oath,' she said to him. 'Now please set me free and give your consent to my marrying this man to whom I am betrothed. And take this gold and silver as your reward.'

"The young man gave his consent and released the girl from her undertaking, saying that, since she had been faithful to her oath, he would set her free and not stand in the way of her marriage. But the gold and silver he refused to take, and he bade the couple depart in peace. On their way home, they were waylaid by a band of brigands, the chief of whom was an old man. They seized all the couple's money and the bride's jewels, and the old man wanted to take the girl as his wife. She then told him her story, saying: 'If a youth in the full vigor of life controlled his passion for me and refused to take my gold, how much more should you, an old and venerable man, be filled with the fear of God and bridle your passion. Let me and my betrothed go our way in peace.' The brigand chief, heeding the girl's plea, returned the money and the jewels and let the couple go.

"This," concluded Solomon, "is the matter I wanted to put to you. Who of all the persons concerned acted in the most noble manner? Tell me whose behavior, in your opinion, was the most praiseworthy."

Said the first merchant: "I praise the girl because she was faithful to her oath."

"Nay," retorted the second, "it is clear that the old brigand acted the most nobly since, contrary to the habits of those who follow his calling, he returned the money and the jewels and let the betrothed couple continue on their way."

"I praise them both," said the third litigant. "The youth behaved most nobly, but I think him a fool not to have taken the gold and silver offered him."

"Ah!" observed Solomon, "it is plain that you are the person who stole your companions' money, for you have acted as witness against yourself. If your mind is on the riches you have not seen, and you think the noble youth a fool because he refused to accept the money, how much more must you have lusted after the money you did see."

Solomon then ordered the man to be thrown into a dungeon. The thief confessed to his crime and indicated the place where he had concealed the gold and silver.

The Wisdom
and Folly of Women

Introduction

In Jewish life and tradition, the woman has always played a central role. The life of the household revolves around her, and from her the family draws its strength and comfort. Since early times in Israelite history, women have taken prominent parts in the fortunes of the tribe and the nation. Their names are recorded in the pages of Biblical history: the matriarchs—the mothers of the nation—Sarah, Rebecca, Rachel, Leah; Deborah, the great tribal heroine of Israel, whose celebrated song of triumph is one of the earliest examples of Hebrew poetry; Ruth, the Moabitess, who became the ancestress of the House of David; Hannah, who, after praying to God for a man child, bore Samuel and gave him to the service of God; Huldah, the prophetess, who flourished in the latter days of the Kingdom of Judah; Esther, who is honored at the Festival of Purim.

Yet in spite of the exalted position of women in Judaism, they suffered a number of inequities in Hebrew law. For example, they were not considered competent witnesses in either criminal or civil cases. While stories abound in popular Jewish literature about pious and virtuous women and their deeds, there is no lack of stories, anecdotes, and proverbs portraying women as faithless and deceitful liars, gossips, creatures in whom no trust should be

placed. More often than not, the tellers of these tales were con-
firmed misogynists and considered it their duty, no doubt, to warn
the unwary against the wiles of women. Some of these accounts
were detailed in a spirit of good-humored tolerance or contempt,
others with malice and venom.

In this section are a simple story of a charitable and virtuous
deed miraculously rewarded (page 94); a tale of a hard-working
widow miraculously delivered from a grim death (page 100); another of a chaste spouse who withstands temptation (page 97);
and still another of a merchant's wife, made of weaker clay, who
succumbs (page 102).

Perhaps the most interesting of these tales is the first, "The
Clever Peasant Girl" (page 89), taken from *The Book of Delight*
by Joseph ben Meir ibn Zabara. It contains two or three stories
rolled into one—the familiar themes of dream interpretation, the
solving of riddles, and the reading of signs—and is reminiscent of
a similar tale in Tunisian folklore. Weak and strong, shrewd and
cunning, women are pictured in all their facets in the Jewish tale.

The Clever Peasant Girl

There was once a wise and mighty king who had many wives and concubines. One night he dreamed that he saw an ape of the Yemen leap onto the necks of the women of his harem. When he awoke in the morning he was much troubled, and his strength seemed departed from his body. He said to himself: "Surely this can be no other than the king of the Yemen, who will come and drive me from my kingdom and seize my wives and concubines for himself."

When the king arose from his bed, one of the palace eunuchs, who was his chamberlain, saw that his royal master was disturbed and ill at ease. He asked the king the cause.

The king replied: "I dreamed a dream in which I tasted the bitterness of death. Do you perchance know of anyone in this land skilled in the interpretation of dreams?"

"Yes, my lord," answered the eunuch. "I have heard that there is a wise man living three days' journey from this place who has knowledge of many things and is a skilled interpreter of dreams, however deep and obscure. Tell me your dream, and I will go to him." So the king related his dream and bade the eunuch set out in search of this wise man. The eunuch thereupon mounted his mule and set off. On his way he fell in with a peasant riding on an ass.

The eunuch greeted him, saying, "Peace be with you, O worker of the earth, who yourself are earth and eat earth." The peasant laughed at these words. "Where are you going?" asked the eunuch.

"To my house," the other replied.

"We are going the same way. Will you carry me, or shall I carry you?" the eunuch went on.

"My lord," answered the peasant, "how can I carry you since you are riding your mule and I am riding my ass?"

They rode along in silence until they came to a field full of wheat. The peasant exclaimed, "How beautiful is this field, and how full are the ears of wheat!" to which the eunuch rejoined, "If the wheat be not already eaten."

Farther on, the riders came to a tall, strongly fortified tower built upon a rock. Said the peasant, "Behold this lofty tower; how fine is its appearance and how well fortified!" to which the eunuch added, "It is indeed fortified without, if it be not destroyed within." After a while he observed: "There is snow on the height." The peasant laughed at this remark, for it was the month of Tammuz in high summer and there was no snow anywhere in the world.

They rode farther and came to a road on both sides of which wheat was growing.

"Upon this road," said the eunuch, "there has passed a horse blind in one eye, carrying a load with oil on one side and vinegar on the other."

They continued their journey and, as they were approaching a city, they passed a funeral procession. The eunuch asked, "Is the man they are carrying dead or alive?" The peasant thought, "How can this person look so wise when, in truth, he is one of the most stupid of people?"

At sunset the eunuch inquired of the peasant whether there was a place nearby where he could lodge for the night. "Yes," said the peasant, "there is a village in front of us where I live. Do me the honor, my lord, of coming to my home. I have both straw and provender."

"I grant your request to do what pleases you, and will enter your house as you ask."

The eunuch entered the man's house and ate and drank and fed his mule; then he lay down to sleep. The peasant and his wife and two daughters also went to bed. At midnight the peasant woke up and aroused his wife and daughters to tell them of his meeting with the eunuch. "How stupid a man our guest is," he said. "He met me on the road and wearied me all day with his talk and strange sayings."

"What makes you think him a fool?" asked the peasant's wife. In reply her husband told her about his saying, "Will you carry me or shall I carry you?" and his strange remarks about the wheatfield, the tower, the snow on the height, the road, the funeral party, and the eunuch's greeting him as one who ate the earth. The peasant grew more loquacious as he related his story, for he thought that the eunuch was asleep. He did not know that the latter was awake and listening to every word. When the peasant had finished talking, his younger daughter, a girl of fifteen, spoke.

"Indeed, father," she said, "our guest is a wise and knowledgeable man. It is you who do not understand him properly. You did not understand the import of his words, for he spoke out of his wisdom and knowledge of many things. When he spoke of a worker of earth and an eater of earth, his meaning was that all that man eats comes forth from the earth. In truth, you yourself are earth, for is it not said, 'From dust you are come; to dust you shall return'? As for his words, 'Will you carry me, or shall I carry you?' they meant that everyone who travels with a companion and entertains him with stories and witty conversation thereby carries his companion, and relieves him of the weariness of the journey and banishes troubling thoughts. And as for the field of wheat, the eunuch spoke truly, for its owner may be poor and already may have received the price of the grain in advance, or perhaps may have borrowed on the security of the grain before it was harvested. The remarks about the tower signify that a house without food or drink in it is destroyed from within and shelters nothing save fear of starvation. When the eunuch spoke of snow upon the height, he meant that your beard is white. You should have answered, 'Aye, time has made it so.' And the horse which was blind in one eye? The eunuch may have perceived this from the fact that the grass on one side of the road was eaten, whereas that on the other side was untouched. How did he know about the oil and vinegar? He observed that the vinegar had dried out in the dust but the oil had not. His question about the dead body was likewise meaningful, for if the deceased had left a son to succeed him, he is, in truth, alive; if he did not, then he is dead."

When morning came, the maiden said to her father: "Before the stranger departs, set before him the food I am about to give you." Thereupon she gave her father thirty eggs, a bowl of milk, and a whole loaf of bread, saying, "Go and ask our guest how many days are wanting of the month, whether the moon is full or not, and whether the sun is whole."

The peasant took the food, but first he ate two of the eggs and a little of the bread and drank some of the milk. The remainder he gave to the eunuch, and asked the questions as his daughter had bidden him.

"Tell your daughter," replied the eunuch, "that the sun is not whole, nor the moon full, and the month wants two days to its completion."

The peasant laughed at this, and said to his daughter, "Did I not tell you that this man is simple? We are in mid-month, yet he says but two days are wanting."

"Father," said the girl, "did you eat some of the food I gave you?"

"Yes," replied the peasant, "I ate two of the eggs and a little bread, and I drank some of the milk."

"Now," said the daughter, "I know beyond all doubt that this man is truly wise and of great understanding."

When the eunuch heard this exchange between father and daughter, he marveled at the wisdom of the girl and asked her father's permission to speak to her. This the peasant readily granted. The eunuch addressed the girl, questioned and examined her, and found her quick-witted and intelligent. He then disclosed the purpose of his journey and told father and daughter about the king's dream. When the eunuch had finished talking, the girl said:

"I shall interpret the meaning of the king's dream, but to him only; to no other person will I reveal it." The eunuch begged the girl's father and mother to allow her to accompany him back, for should she go with him his honor and glory would be increased. The peasant feared the king, his sovereign, so he gave his daughter permission to go, saying, "Let my lord do that which is good in his sight."

That same morning, the maiden set off in the company of the eunuch, who took her before the king and related to his royal master all that had befallen him. He told him that the peasant's daughter would interpret the dream if she could speak to him alone. The king looked upon the girl with favor, and had her conducted to one of the royal apartments where he related his dream.

"Fear not, my lord the king," said the peasant girl, "what took place in your dream, because you will have peace; the dream has no evil portent for the kingdom. Yet, withal, I fear to declare its interpretation lest it cast shame upon the king."

"Have no fear, and do not be ashamed to interpret my dream, for there is no other man with me," said the king. So the girl spoke.

"Let my lord the king search among his wives and maidservants and concubines, and he will find among them a young man attired as a woman. He lies with them, and he is the ape the king saw leaping on their necks in the dream."

So the king searched among his wives and concubines, and found in their midst a youth of surpassing beauty, comely in form and feature, and taller than all those around him. The king seized hold of him and slew him. Afterward he had the faithless women put to death. He took the peasant's daughter as his wife and placed the royal crown upon her head. He then swore an oath and vowed that never as long as she lived would he take another woman to wife.

The Charitable Woman and the Three Loaves

During the reign of King Solomon, son of David—peace be upon them both!—there lived a poor but charitable woman who was ever ready to do good toward those less fortunate than herself. Every day she baked three loaves of bread. Two of these she distributed among the poor, keeping the third for herself. One day a stranger came to her door and begged her for some food.

"I am tired and hungry," he said, "for I have not tasted any food for three whole days. I was sailing aboard a vessel with all my goods and possessions when a storm arose and sank the boat. All others aboard were drowned, but I was washed ashore by the waves and saved from death."

On hearing his story, the good woman at once fetched one of her loaves and gave it to the starving man. As she was about to eat one of the three loaves herself, another stranger appeared at her door.

"Good woman," he said, "I was captured by my enemies but managed to escape them three days ago. Since that time I have not had a morsel of food. Please take pity on me and give me a piece of bread that I may not die of starvation!"

Moved by his plea, the charitable woman immediately handed the man the loaf she was about to eat, praising God for granting her the opportunity to feed the hungry and the needy. She then took the third and last remaining loaf and prepared to eat it herself, when yet another man appeared and begged for a morsel to eat. "On the road," he told her, "I was seized by robbers but managed to escape from them into a forest. For three days I have been obliged to exist on roots and herbs. Give me a piece of bread, I beg you, for I am faint with hunger."

Without hesitation the pious woman offered him the third loaf, leaving nothing for herself. She went to the sack for more flour to bake another loaf but found it empty. She thereupon went out to the fields to gather some wheat. After collecting a few grains, she carried them to a mill and had them ground into flour which she then put into her small sack. On her way home, a gust of wind blew up suddenly, snatching the sack and carrying it off into the distance. She returned home empty-handed and had no bread for the rest of the day. In bitterness and despair, the poor woman cried out: "O Lord of the universe! What wrong have I committed that I should be so punished?"

Bewildered, she went to King Solomon to complain of her misfortune. It so happened that on that day the king had called a meeting of the high council, so the woman addressed herself to all its members.

"Tell me, O you judges of Israel," she cried, "why the Lord has punished me in this manner, seeing that I gave food to the hungry and yet am now compelled to suffer the pangs of hunger myself?"

As she was thus speaking, three merchants who had disembarked from their vessel entered the council chamber and, standing before Solomon, said, "Our lord the king, take from us these seven thousand gold pieces and distribute them as charity among the noble and deserving poor."

Surprised at this gesture, the king asked the merchants why they were so anxious to give away such a large sum of money. They replied:

"As we were approaching the shore, our ship, which was carrying a valuable cargo of merchandise, sprung a leak. We cast around for something to stop up the hole but could find nothing. The boat was sinking and we seemed doomed to drown with all our goods. In our terror and distress we prayed to God, crying out, 'Creator of the universe! If we should reach the shore in safety, we vow that we will give away to the poor a tenth part of the value of our merchandise.' We then prostrated ourselves in prayer and awaited our fate in silence. So great was our despair and our distress that we failed to observe that the ship had meanwhile reached the shore safely. We then calculated the exact value of our merchandise and found that a tenth part of it came to seven thousand gold pieces. Hence, in fulfillment of our vow, we now bring you the money that you may distribute it among the poor."

Thereupon the wise Solomon asked the merchants if they knew the exact spot where their vessel had sprung its leak, and whether they knew how the hole had been plugged. When they replied that they did not know, the king said, "Go back then and examine the vessel."

Thereupon, the merchants left the king's presence and returned soon afterwards carrying a small flour sack. "This sack," they told him, "had, all unbeknown to us, stopped up the hole in our vessel."

The king turned to the pious woman and asked her if she recognized the flour sack.

"Indeed I do," was the woman's reply. "It's the sack I was carrying on my head when a gust of wind snatched it and bore it off."

"Then take the seven thousand gold pieces as your reward for your good deeds. It was for your sake that God wrought this miracle. He does not forsake those who walk in His ways and follow His commandments."

And all those present wondered at the great wisdom of Solomon, king of Israel.

The Craftsman's Wife

When King Solomon was about to build the Temple in Jerusalem, he dispatched messengers to the kings and princes of neighboring countries, asking them to send their most skillful workers to the land of Israel. The rulers of these countries, complying with Solomon's request, sent their finest artisans and craftsmen.

But it happened that in a certain town there was one master craftsman who refused to journey to Jerusalem, despite the high rewards offered for working there. His reason was that he had a wife of surpassing beauty, and he feared to leave her lest she be tempted to be unfaithful to him.

When the king of his country heard that one of his subjects had refused to go to Jerusalem to work on the Temple, he called the master craftsman before him.

"You must go at once to Jerusalem," he commanded. "King Solomon is a mighty ruler, and I dare not refuse his request."

With a heavy heart the master craftsman went home and told his wife what had happened. "Do not grieve on my account," said the woman. "I will give you a talisman which will show you a sign should I abandon the path of virtue. Obey the king's command and go now to Jerusalem. Be of good cheer, and fear nothing."

Before the husband set out on his journey, his wife gave him a tiny glass tube containing a piece of cotton and a glowing coal.

So long as the piece of cotton did not catch fire, she told him, he could be assured that she had not betrayed him. The master craftsman then hung the talisman round his neck and departed for the Holy City.

One day while the man was working on the Temple building, King Solomon, who used to visit the site regularly, caught sight of the strange talisman and asked its owner its significance. The man told him his reason for wearing it.

Solomon went away thinking of the matter. He then called two handsome strongly-built youths and ordered them to journey to the town where the master craftsman lived. He told them to take lodgings in his house and seduce the man's wife. After arriving in the town, the two young men took lodgings with the woman and made themselves agreeable to her. She treated them hospitably and prepared food for them. After the meal she led them to the room she had readied for them. As soon as they entered, she locked the door and kept them imprisoned there for a month.

Meanwhile, King Solomon continued to visit the Temple site daily, and every day he watched the talisman hung round the craftsman's neck, but the piece of cotton never caught fire. Greatly surprised, Solomon one day resolved to go to that town himself as an ordinary traveler, and with two servants to attend him he journeyed to the woman's house and took lodgings there. The craftsman's wife, who possessed wisdom as well as beauty, guessed at once that the stranger was the king of Israel. She cooked him a number of dishes and then placed before him a plate of hard-boiled eggs painted in different colors. "Taste these eggs, my lord the king," she said.

Solomon, greatly surprised, asked why she had addressed him as king.

"Your dignity is that of a king and your deportment that of a great ruler," replied the woman. "I am but your humble handmaid. I pray you, my lord, eat these eggs and tell me how is their taste."

Solomon ate a little of every egg on the plate, then said, "All these eggs taste alike: none differs from the other."

"So it is with us women," said the craftsman's wife. "We are only differently painted. Was it worth your majesty's while to make such a long journey for the sake of a pretty face? Do with me what you will, for I am your servant; but know that in the end all earthly pleasures are fleeting and all unlawful desires vain and sinful."

At the humble woman's words Solomon exclaimed: "Blessed be you to God and blessed all those of pure heart."

Before his departure he left the woman a costly gift and praised her for her steadfastness and faithfulness in the face of temptation. On his return to Jerusalem, Solomon called the craftsman before him and related all that had happened. He paid him tenfold for his work in the building of the Temple and bade him return home in peace.

The Pious Washerwoman

There once lived in Jerusalem a pious woman who had lost her husband. She supported herself and her children by taking in washing. Among the rich neighbors for whom she did work was the keeper of David's tomb.

One day this man came to her and said, "You are a good and righteous woman, and you toil all the day washing clothes in order to support your family. As a reward I shall permit you to visit the tomb of King David—peace be upon him!—which no Jew has been allowed to enter to this day." The poor widow was overjoyed and thanked the keeper profusely.

The next day he took the woman to the tomb, led her to the gate of a passage, and told her to go through. She did so, but hardly had she entered than the man quickly shut and locked the gate, leaving her alone in the darkness. He then went to the *qadi* (Muslim judge) and told him that a Jewish woman had entered the tomb of David, knowing that it was forbidden to do so, and that he—the keeper—had locked her in. In a rage at this profanation, the *qadi* ordered that the woman be let out and put to death for her crime.

The unfortunate woman realized too late that the evil keeper had betrayed her and that her life was in danger. Terror-stricken, she prostrated herself and prayed to God to have pity on her for the sake of His servant David. As she was praying and lamenting her fate, a great light suddenly illuminated the interior of the tomb, and she beheld standing before her a white-haired old man of commanding appearance looking down at her with compassion. Drawing the frightened woman to her feet, he led her by the hand and guided her through many winding passages until they reached the open.

"Return speedily to your house," said the old man, "and do not tarry on the way. Take up your washing and start your work again and tell no person what happened to you." And with these words he vanished.

Meanwhile, the *qadi,* accompanied by his men, arrived at the gate of the tomb and ordered that the woman be seized and put to death. But neither the *qadi* nor his men could find any trace of the washerwoman in the tomb, though they searched it many times. In anger, the *qadi* turned on the keeper and accused him of having played a trick on him. But the latter swore oaths that the woman had entered the tomb, for had he not locked her in? The *qadi* thereupon sent one of his servants to the washerwoman's house. The servant soon returned and informed his master that he had found the woman washing clothes.

The keeper did not know what to say. He was charged by the *qadi* with perjury and sentenced to death. The pious washerwoman said nothing about the miracle that had taken place in the tomb of King David until she was on her deathbed, when she revealed the secret to the rabbis and community of the Holy City.

The Merchant's Wife

A king had an argument one day with some of his counselors about the virtues of women. The counselors sang their praises and spoke of the great wisdom and patience of women. But the king disagreed. "Restrain your words," he told them. "Never has one heard of women who are good and virtuous and endowed with knowledge and understanding. They can think only of themselves and their own pleasure." The counselors, however, were not to be convinced. They pointed out to the monarch that there were women who were both wise and understanding, virtuous and faithful. "They love and honor their husbands," they said, "manage well their households, and look after their sons and daughters." To which the king replied that he would prove the truth of his observations. He challenged the counselors to find in the city a single woman endowed with the qualities and virtues of which they spoke. The counselors sought and found a woman of great reputation, modest, virtuous and wise, and of surpassing beauty. Her husband was a prosperous merchant of blameless reputation.

The king sent for the husband and told him that he had a matter of secrecy to discuss with him.

"I have a daughter, my only child," said the king, "who is as good as she is beautiful. I have no wish to give her in marriage to a prince or a nobleman. I seek a good and faithful man, one free from the evil of the times, so that he may cherish and honor her and maintain her with lovingkindness. It has come to my knowledge that you are a man of excellent qualities and good character, and as such would be a fine husband for my daughter. But I cannot give her to any man who already has a wife; therefore, I tell you, you must kill your wife this very night, and on the morrow I will give you my daughter in marriage."

The merchant protested. "Who am I," he asked, "that I should be the son-in-law of a king? Indeed, I am not worthy to tend your sheep."

"I choose you," replied the king, "because you are dear to me; without you no man shall raise his hand or his foot in all my kingdom."

But the merchant still hesitated. "My lord," he said, "how can I slay my wife who has been my companion these fifteen years? She is my joy and delight; she shares my food and drink. She loves and honors me and watches over me and ministers to my welfare." But the king would not listen. "Hearken to me," he commanded, "and slay her, for by her death great honor will be yours. I will raise you above all the nobles of my kingdom and you will rule over all."

"I shall try and see if I can do this base deed," said the man. With which he left the king's presence, his heart heavy with sadness and grief.

When he got home, his wife greeted him with pleasure, which only served to increase the poor man's distress. Seeing her husband's mournful face, the wife asked him why he looked so sad. But the merchant refrained from telling her and said instead, "May the Almighty guard you from death and destruction; there is nothing wrong and nothing ails me."

That same night, as his wife lay deep in slumber, the merchant rose from his bed in a confused state of mind, with the intention of carrying out the king's orders. His sword in his right hand and a lamp in his left, he pulled the bed-covering from his wife. But as he beheld her peacefully sleeping with their two children, his resolve faded, and he took pity on her, saying to himself: "Woe is me! How can I kill her? Where will I hide my shame? Who will bring up my children, the apples of my eye? Surely this has happened because of the multitude of my sins and transgressions." So saying, he returned the sword to its sheath; his heart was overcome with remorse, and he wept. "My wife is better than all the kingdoms," he vowed. "Cursed be all kings, for they do but pursue their own desires and seduce the ears of men with their vanities." He then got back into bed.

The following morning he went to his warehouse as usual to transact the day's business. Awaiting him there were the king's messengers, sent to take him before the king. When the merchant saw them his heart sank and he began to tremble with fear. The king asked if he had slain his wife as he had been commanded.

"No, my lord the king," was the reply, "for my love and pity for her overcame me and I could not do this deed." He thereupon related all that had happened when he took his sword to strike her. When the king heard this, he became angry and shouted, "Get out of my sight and never look upon my face again! For you are in no wise a man, but a woman with the heart of a woman." The merchant left the king's presence, greatly relieved despite the king's anger and harsh words.

In the evening of the same day the king sent one of his servants to fetch the merchant's wife in secret. As the king gazed on the face of the woman, he marveled at her comeliness and beauty. He then addressed her, "I have heard much of your wisdom and seemly conduct, and from that day my heart has not ceased to burn for love of you. I wish to make you my wife and give you my kingdom as a heritage. But since I cannot take a woman who is already married, you must go and kill your husband this very night. Once you have done that, I will take you and do for you all that your heart desires."

The woman's heart swelled with joy, and she replied, "I shall do what the king wishes and shall become his handmaid." And the

king said: "Nay, you shall be my wife, and all my wives and concubines shall be your servants and handmaidens." With those
words the king gave the merchant's wife a sword forged of tin, for
he knew the weakness of a woman's wit. "Here is my sword," he
said, "a blade exceedingly keen. Smite your husband with it but
once; there will be no need to strike a second time, for he will rise
no more." The woman took the sword and went back to her house
rejoicing.

She prepared a repast of meats and mixed wines and set the
meal up ready for her husband's arrival. When the merchant returned home, he sat down to eat and drink with his sons and his
wife. She made him drink an excess of wine until he became
drunk, after which she lifted him to his bed and laid him down.
During the night, while he was still in a drunken slumber, she
rose and, taking the sword, smote the sleeping man hard on the
head, thinking that the weapon would pierce him and kill him.
But the tin sword bent back, and he awoke from his sleep, shout-
ing: "Who has roused me from my sleep and struck me on the
head?"

When the woman saw that he was awake and that the sword
blow had left him unharmed, she trembled with fear and dismay
and her heart grew faint. She said: "Fear not, my beloved, lie
down and go back to sleep; perhaps you dreamed you saw someone striking you." So the man went back to sleep quickly, for the
influence of the wine was still on him. But his wife's anxiety and
fear grew. She waited trembling until the dawn broke, when she
got up to go about her household tasks, and to atone for the evil
deed she had wrought. She set about preparing some food for her
husband according to her habit.

The king, meanwhile, awaited her coming, and when she did not
present herself at the palace, he sent for her.

"Have you done the deed agreed upon between us, or did you
take pity on him?" asked the king.

The woman replied: "My lord, I did your bidding, but you frus-
trated my plan and it came to naught; for when I raised your

sword against him I found it useless for its task." And she related to the king what she had done. Then the king sent for the woman's husband and bade him tell the king's wise men about his orders to kill his wife and what had happened. The king then bade the woman tell the wise men of her attempt to kill her husband, and she did so.

Then the king spoke to his counselors and said: "Surely, this is the meaning of the words I spoke when I told you to restrain your words."

And the wise men marveled at the king's wisdom.

The Righteous
and the Pious

Introduction

The stories in this section all teach a moral or point a lesson. Their theme is that if a person pursues the path of righteousness and obeys God's laws and commandments, he will suffer no harm or evil but will be "delivered out of trouble."

In the first story (page 111), which has for its title part of a verse from the book of Proverbs, the hero is a young man who is protected against evil by heeding the command of his dying father never to pass a synagogue without entering, and never to leave a place of worship before the completion of the service. Many variations of this story exist. One version, for example, has it that Maimonides, the intended victim of an angry king, was saved by stopping at a synagogue and then attending a circumcision ceremony at a poor man's house.

"The Righteous Heir" (page 114) belongs to the popular "judgment of Solomon" type of tale in which the judge has to decide between the conflicting claims of two persons. In "Leviathan and the Dutiful Son" (page 125), which is really a fable and embodies more than one story, the message is simple: filial piety leads to prosperity and reward. "The Divided Cloak" (page 123), a less common type, is another variation on this theme: here a young man teaches his father a gentle lesson in filial piety—that is, to show to his own father, the youth's grandfather, the love and respect due him.

"The Righteous Is Delivered Out of Trouble and the Wicked Comes in His Stead" *

There once lived a pious man who had a son of handsome appearance and noble bearing. Before he died, the father admonished his son never, on any account, to leave a place of worship before all the prayers had been recited. He also commanded the youth that, should he pass a synagogue and hear the voice of the reader, he was to enter the building and stay there until the service was ended.

After the death of the pious man, the son was appointed chief steward in the royal palace. His task was to serve wine to members of the royal household, prepare their meals, and look after the table. He carried out his duties to the satisfaction of his master, the sovereign, and led an upright life, carrying out the instructions of his lamented father. The young man enjoyed the respect of all in the palace save the vizier—the king's chief minister. He hated the youth and one day went to the king and accused the chief steward of being the queen's lover. His royal master was at first loath to believe his vizier but in the end was persuaded that the latter spoke the truth. Then the monarch's anger and jealousy knew no bounds, and he set himself to think of some means of de-

* Proverbs 11:8.

111

stroying the young man.

It so happened that one day the king was passing by the royal lime-kilns when he was struck with an idea. He summoned the foreman of the kilns and said: "The first person to pass by this kiln tomorrow morning as my messenger is to be cast immediately into the furnace. See that my bidding is carried out; otherwise you will be severely punished." The foreman promised to do as he was commanded.

That evening the king summoned the youth to his apartment and told him that on the morrow he was to rise early, go to the lime-kilns, and instruct the foreman, in the king's name, to heat the furnace to higher temperatures than usual. The following morning the youth rose early, saddled a horse, and rode out to the lime-kilns to carry out the king's orders. On the way, however, he passed a synagogue and heard the precentor intoning the morning service. Heedful of his late father's admonition, the young man dismounted and entered the house of prayer and remained there until the service was over. He then continued on to the lime-kilns.

Meanwhile, unaware of what had been going on, the king summoned the vizier and ordered him to go without delay to the lime-kilns and check to see if the foreman had carried out the royal command. No sooner did the vizier appear than he was seized, at the behest of the foreman, and thrown into the furnace. At almost the same instant, the young man arrived, in time to witness the fate of the unfortunate vizier. Astonished at the sight, he asked the foreman why he had committed this evil deed.

"I have done no more than carry out the king's command," the foreman replied, "for he ordered me to throw the first person who appeared into the furnace, and I have done so."

The young man returned to the palace and presented himself before the king, who was greatly astonished at seeing him alive. In a rage he cried out: "You did not obey my command!"

"Sire," replied the puzzled youth, "I did as you bade me and went to the lime-kilns. But when I arrived there to carry out the royal order I found that the vizier had been cast into the furnace."

When he heard these words the king was afraid, and he was seized with trembling. He looked at the young man before him. Then he said:

"Now do I perceive that you are an upright and Godfearing person. My vizier spoke evil of you and turned me against you, and I, in the heat of my anger, ordered the foreman of the lime-kilns to cast into the furnace the first person who should appear in the morning. So I sent you at an early hour, and after a while I sent the vizier to make sure my instructions had been carried out. Because you tarried on the way, the man who bore false witness against you has met death in your place."

The Righteous Heir

There once lived a merchant of great wealth who owned vast possessions and many slaves and servants, but who had only one child, a son. When the boy reached manhood, he asked his father to let him travel to far-off countries so that he might trade and learn something of the customs and wisdom of foreign peoples. The father granted the young man's wish and equipped him with merchandise and gold and silver. The son soon set sail, leaving his father alone except for a favorite slave whom the old man treated as a member of the family rather than a servant. This slave was industrious and shrewd and gained the trust of his master. One day the rich merchant died suddenly, leaving no will or testament concerning the disposal of his possessions. Without delay the servant seized his late master's property and his gold and silver, and used it as though he had the title and right to it. As the time passed, people no longer knew whether the inheritor was a slave or the son of the dead merchant.

After ten years had passed, the real son and true heir returned home from his travels. The vessel on which he had sailed had been filled with his many possessions, for he had traded in many lands and acquired vast wealth. One day, however, a storm had blown up and the ship had sprung a leak, and the passengers had been forced to throw all their merchandise overboard in order to lighten the vessel. But it had been to no avail; in the end all aboard had had to abandon ship and save their lives as best they could. The merchant's son had managed to swim and reach the shore.

After walking many miles, barefooted, with his clothes in tatters, he arrived at his house. When he learned that his father had died, he claimed his rightful inheritance but was beaten and driven away from his home by the former slave, who claimed that the house now belonged to him. In his sorrow and distress, the son went to a certain clever judge and related all that had happened. "He has seized all my late father's possessions," he cried, "and driven me out of the house that is rightfully mine!"

The judge then ordered the one-time slave to appear before him, and when the latter stood in his presence, the judge felt sure that he was a person capable of any base and evil deed. "Is it true," the judge asked, "that the house you now live in and the property you possess once belonged to your father? For this man claims that you are no more than a slave with no right or title to his father's wealth."

"It is true, my lord," replied the usurper, "that the deceased was my revered father, for whom I still mourn. I am his only son, to whom he bequeathed his wealth and possessions."

"Have you any reliable witnesses who will prove that you are in truth the son and heir of the deceased?" asked the judge. "My lord," answered the crafty slave, "I stand accused, and it is for my accuser, this lying person here, to bring witnesses who can testify that he is the deceased man's son and rightful heir."

The judge ordered both men to go and seek witnesses who would be able to testify to their respective claims, but neither could find any person able to prove his identity. All who had once known them either were dead or no longer lived in that place. So they both returned to the judge and told him they were unable to find witnesses. "It is for our lord the judge," they said, "to find the truth and give judgment accordingly."

The judge pondered for a few moments, then turned to the two men and asked, "Does either of you know where the grave of the deceased merchant is?"

Replied the slave, "I know it well, for, as his son, did I not bury him?" The judge then ordered his attendants to go to the grave which the slave had promised to show them. "Disinter the corpse of that misguided man," bade the judge, "and bring his bones before me that I may burn them; for he did wrong in not leaving any will or testament, which is the cause of all this disputing and mischief."

The usurping slave at once agreed. "My lord," he said, "I will open the grave of the deceased without delay and bring you the bones. Well have you spoken and given judgment like an angel of the Lord."

But when the real son heard these words, he wept and cried out, "No, my lord, let this man keep my father's wealth. I am ready to renounce my claim rather than have the author of my days be dragged from his last resting place."

Thereupon the wise judge said, "You have indeed proved yourself to be the son and rightful heir of the dead man. I give judgment in your favor, for you are the rightful owner of your father's possessions, while the other person is only a slave and usurper."

The Pious Butcher

There once lived a man honest and righteous in all his actions. It so happened that he lived in a street which was on the route to a cemetery, so that all funeral processions on their way to the burial-ground had to pass his house. Whenever this happened, this man would follow the procession to the cemetery and pray for the soul of the departed. One day, however, the righteous man became ill and weak in his limbs, and he was unable to rise to his feet and walk. That day was the funeral of a just and respected citizen, but the righteous man was not able to accompany the hearse to the burial-place, and he was much grieved, so he prayed to God, saying:

"O Lord of the universe, who restores sight to the blind and causes the lame to walk, You, who have made my limbs feeble, hearken to my prayer and grant me the strength to rise from my bed and accompany every pious and upright person to his final resting place." And a messenger of the Lord appeared to the man in a vision and said: "The Lord has heard your prayer and granted your request." And so, whenever a pious and upright citizen died and the procession was passing the house of the afflicted man, the latter miraculously regained the use of his legs and was thus able to follow the hearse and pray for the departed.

One day a man known throughout the town as upright and God-fearing died, and at the appointed time his hearse passed the righteous cripple's house on its way to the cemetery. The man at once prepared to rise and accompany the procession but found that he could not move his limbs. On the following day another funeral passed his house: it was that of a butcher, a man known as a disputatious person and a bad character given to evil ways. To the surprise of all, the cripple was able to rise from his bed and follow the cortège. The people wondered how it was that the invalid should have found strength to rise from his bed and follow the hearse of the dead butcher, and yet had been unable to do so in the case of the Godfearing and upright man the day before. "Perhaps after all," they said, "the butcher may not have been the evil-doer we thought him."

Two wise old men resolved to look into the matter and find the reason for these strange happenings. They first went to see the butcher's widow and asked her about the conduct of her departed husband. She told them of his quarrelsome ways and evil deeds and his transgressions against the commandments. "But," she said, "he had one virtue. He had an aged father a hundred years old whom he honored and served all the days of his life. He kissed the old man's hand every day and dressed and undressed him and tended him with loving care. Daily he took him the marrow from the bones of the sheep and oxen he had slaughtered and from it prepared delicate food for the old man."

Having heard the words of the butcher's widow, her two interlocutors now realized that in virtue of his respect and solicitude for his aged parent, the butcher had sufficiently atoned for his evil-doing and transgressions, and had departed this world free of sin. The two sages then visited the house of the Godfearing man for whom the cripple had been unable to rise from his bed, and asked his widow about her late husband. The widow wept at his memory and told the two visitors that her late husband had been a pious and upright man who dealt kindly with her, their children and the servants. "Three times a day," she wept, "he recited his prayers and walked in the ways of the Lord. Even at midnight he used to get up from his bed and retire to a room where he continued to pray and meditate."

When the two visitors asked the bereaved woman where this room was, she showed them a door that was locked.

"I swear on my life and by the memory of my departed husband that I have never put foot in this room for twenty years," she said. "Neither I nor my children nor any other were allowed to enter this room, for my husband always kept the key with him, carrying it on his breast."

The wise men were curious to know what secret the locked room concealed, so they got the key and opened the door. In the room they found a box containing an image made of gold, an idol which the dead man had worshiped. Thus did they understand that the deceased had abandoned the true faith while publicly making himself out to be a Godfearing and pious person. Thus was the dead man like one of those who do the deeds of Zimri yet hope for the reward of Pinḥas.*

* See Numbers 25, which tells the story of the zealous Godfearing Pinḥas and the evil-doing Zimri.

Akiba and the Daughter of Kalba Sabbu'a

Rabbi Akiba * began his life as a very poor man and ended it as a very rich one, and for this he had his wife to thank. It is said that he had a crown made, set with precious stones, for his wife, and when his children asked why he gave their mother such a valuable present, he answered that he could never adequately repay her for all she had done for him.

It happened this way. Rabbi Akiba's wife, Rachel, was the daughter of one Kalba Sabbu'a, one of the richest men in the city of Jerusalem, while Akiba was a shepherd who tended her father's flock. She refused to marry a rich man and instead married Akiba, but on condition that he apply himself to study. As a result, she was driven penniless from the house by her father and went to live with Akiba's mother. Since she had to earn a living, she went to work secretly (since no daughter of Kalba Sabbu'a could be seen working in public) and sent part of her earnings to her husband, who was studying. One day a lame man, who knew what was happening, laughed and said mockingly: "Her hair will be gray before

* Palestinian teacher (50 C.E. to 132 C.E.), known as the father of rabbinic Judaism. He was put to death by the Romans because he defied Hadrian's edict against the practice and teaching of Judaism.

that shepherd ever becomes a scholar!"

It is related by some that Rabbi Akiba was forty years of age when he started to study, and he never believed he would succeed in learning anything. One day, while sitting beside a well, he saw a large stone with a deep groove in its middle. He asked how that had come about and was told that it had been caused by the rope with which a bucket was let down into the well, the rope passing over the stone.

"If such soft material can cut through a stone," Akiba observed, "is there any reason why the words of our Torah, which are hard as iron, should not make an impression on my heart, which is flesh?"

It is said that he used to gather straw daily, half of which he sold to help support himself, and half of which he used to light a fire. His neighbors complained at the smoke caused by his straw fires. One of them said to him, "Akiba, you are choking us with this smoke. Sell us the other half of the straw and buy oil with the money so that you can study by the light of an oil lamp." Akiba retorted, "I can't do that, for I learn, warm myself, and earn my living by the straw."

In time Rabbi Akiba became known for his great scholarship, wisdom, and piety. After the passing of twelve years he returned to Jerusalem with two thousand pupils, and all the people of the Holy City came out to meet him. Among them was Kalba Sabbu'a, who did not recognize him. He asked the great scholar what he should do about his daughter whom he had driven out of his house many years ago and had vowed never to support. Now she must be starving, and he wanted the rabbi to release him from his vow. Rabbi Akiba asked him the reason. "She betrothed herself to an ignorant shepherd who could not even pronounce the benediction over meals."

Akiba then said: "But suppose he has since become a scholar. What then?" And Kalba Sabbu'a replied: "If he just knew how to say the blessing, I would give him half my fortune."

"I am that shepherd," replied Rabbi Akiba. Thereupon his father-in-law greeted him and embraced him and led him to his home, and thanked God for His mercies. When Rabbi Akiba's wife appeared and fell at the feet of her illustrious husband, his pupils, not knowing who she was, tried to push her away, but their master chided them, saying: "Leave her. All that you know and all that I know are due to her. It is the wisdom of women that upholds the house."

The Divided Cloak

A rich man once decided to give all his property and wealth to his son during his lifetime instead of bequeathing it to him after his death. After a while the son took to neglecting his aging father and eventually drove him from his house to fend for himself as best he could. One day the old man, clad in threadbare clothing and shivering in the cold, met his grandson in the street and asked the young man to go to his father and beg him to let the old man have a warm cloak against the winter winds. The young man went home and asked his father to let him have a cloak. After a lot of arguing, the father sent his young son up to a loft at the top of the house and told him to bring down a certain cloak that was hanging there.

The youth ascended to the loft, where he found the cloak. He thereupon took a knife and began to cut the cloak in half. The task took him some time, and his father, wondering at the delay, went up to see what was happening. He asked his son why he was cutting the cloak in half.

"I am giving one half to my grandfather and keeping the other half for his son when he grows old," was the reply.

The man was greatly surprised at the young man's reply. He then realized the wickedness of his deeds toward his aged father and welcomed him back to his house, where he treated him with the honor and deference due him.

Modesty and Wisdom

Rabbi Akiba once had a pearl of very high price to sell, but he could find no one to buy it. As he was walking through the town market with some of his pupils, he was approached by a hungry-looking man in tattered clothes who said that he wanted to buy the pearl at the price asked. He asked the rabbi to accompany him to his house, where he would pay him the money and take the pearl. Akiba was extremely puzzled at this but said nothing; with his pupils he followed the man home. On approaching, they saw a palatial building richly furnished and with many servants. The man took the pearl, paid the money to Rabbi Akiba, and invited him and his pupils to stay for a meal. After they had eaten and drunk their fill, Rabbi Akiba expressed surprise at his host's actions and behavior, and asked their meaning.

"Wealth and riches are not enduring," was the reply. "Today I am rich in worldly possessions. Tomorrow I may lose everything and become a pauper. No man should be proud and boast of his riches. I go about in ragged clothes and keep the company of the poor and the dispossessed so that, should my fortunes suddenly change, I will not be dismayed at my reduced circumstances."

Thereupon Rabbi Akiba blessed his host for his wisdom and modesty.

Leviathan and the Dutiful Son

There once lived a man who used to urge his son to follow the injunction of Koheleth (the preacher), who said: "Cast your bread upon the waters, for you will find it after many days" (Ecclesiastes 11:1).

When his father died, the son remembered his instructions and every day he went to the seashore and threw a piece of bread into the water. Soon, one particular fish began to come regularly every day and eat the bread, and in time it grew larger, stronger, and more powerful than any other fish in the sea. It soon took to oppressing all the other fish, until one day they decided to lay a complaint before Leviathan, king of the waters, and acquaint him with the large fish's tyranny.

"Lord and master," they said, "there is a great fish living with us in these waters who has grown very strong and powerful and is daily oppressing us until we do not know what to do. Every day he swallows a score and more of us, and we poor creatures are powerless against him. We implore your help, O mighty Leviathan!"

The sovereign of the sea at once sent off a messenger and commanded the miscreant to appear before him. But the fish defied his master and swallowed up the royal messenger. Leviathan thereupon dispatched a second messenger, who met with a like fate. Enraged at being thus defied in his own domain, Leviathan decided to go himself to the rebellious fish and chastise him.

"How comes it," he demanded, "that you alone of all the fish of the ocean have grown so strong and powerful that you are able to swallow up your brethren without their being able to withstand you?"

"My lord," was the reply, "I have grown big and strong by virtue of the generosity of a man who dwells on land. Every day he comes with a piece of bread and casts it upon the water and I eat it. Thanks to this daily meal I have grown so strong and mighty that I am able to devour twenty small fish every morning and thirty every evening."

When Leviathan asked him why he ate up his fellow fish, the big fish replied arrogantly: "Because they are slow-witted and dare to oppose me. Is it my fault that they are so stupid as to put themselves within my reach?"

After hearing these words, Leviathan commanded the fish to go and bring the man who came to the shore daily with the piece of bread. The big fish promised to conduct the man to Leviathan's presence on the next day. He then swam to that part of the seashore where his benefactor was in the habit of casting the bread Digging a hole nearby, he hid himself in it and awaited the coming of the young man with his daily portion. When the man came, he fell into the hole and was swallowed up by the fish. The evil-doer then swam back to Leviathan and told him that he had swallowed up and brought the man as promised.

"Spew him forth," ordered Leviathan. And the big fish did as the sea king bade him. He regurgitated the unfortunate fellow, who was immediately swallowed up by Leviathan. "Now tell me," said he to the man inside him, "for what reason you have been throwing a piece of bread into the sea each day."

"In obedience to the teaching of my beloved and revered father," was the reply. Leviathan was pleased with this answer and praised the young man for honoring his father's memory and following his teaching.

"Because of your filial love and respect," said the king of the ocean, "I shall teach you the seventy languages of men and give you knowledge of the tongues of beasts and birds." Whereupon he spewed out the young man a distance of three hundred miles, and the dutiful son found himself in a desolate place where no man had ever before trodden. Bewildered and exhausted, he lay on the ground; suddenly he saw two ravens flying above him and conversing with each other. Having been instructed by Leviathan in the language of the birds, the youth was able to understand what the ravens were saying.

"Father," he heard the younger of the two birds say, "look, there is a man lying on the ground. Is he dead or alive?"

"I do not know," answered the elder raven.

"Then let me descend and tear out his eyes, for I am hungry for a man's eyes."

The father bird advised his son against this, saying that the man on the ground might be alive. But the young bird would not heed his father's advice and swooped down and perched on the man's forehead. As soon as the raven touched him, the man caught hold of the bird's feet and made it captive. The young raven cried out to its father to free it from the young man's grasp.

"Alas!" cried the old raven in distress, "for my miserable and misguided son who refused to listen to his father's counsel." Then the bird turned to the youth and said: "If you understand our speech, listen carefully to my words. Arise and dig the ground beneath you, and you will find there the hidden treasure of our lord, Solomon, king of Israel."

On hearing these words, the youth let the young raven free and began to dig into the ground. The bird had spoken the truth, for it was not long before he came upon the buried treasure. He found precious stones and pearls, and objects of silver and gold. He thus became a wealthy man because Leviathan had taught him the languages of the beasts and birds, and because he had faithfully carried out his father's teaching and cast his bread upon the water.

Tales of
Wit and Wisdom

Introduction

Wit and wisdom constitute the principal themes of the tales that follow. There are also classic examples of craftiness, guile, cunning, cleverness, perception and subtlety.

Perhaps the story of most universal interest is "The Emperor and the Deaf Man" (page 133), dealing with a contest in wisdom between a Christian and a Jew. This belongs to a large group of tales based on the public verbal contests and learned disputations which used to take place between rabbis and priests during the Middle Ages in Europe. They follow a familiar and regular pattern. The emperor or the priest in question gives the heads of the local Jewish community a fixed period—usually a few days—in which to prepare for the contest and select their champions. Failure to do so means misfortune for the Jews. A day of prayer and fasting for the community is ordained, when suddenly, at the last minute, a simple and untutored person appears on the scene, offers to take up the challenge, emerges triumphant, and thus saves the Jews.

Another familiar type of tale is the fable, illustrated here by "Leviathan and the Fox" (page 143). Jews, like so many other people, were bemused by the wily fox.

They were also deeply impressed by the historic figure of Alexander the Great, conqueror of the East, who lived from 356 to 323 B.C.E. He figures prominently in Talmudic, Midrashic, and medieval legend, and is remembered for the privileges he granted the Jews in Palestine and in the Diaspora. By introducing Hellenic culture into Egypt and Syria, it is said, he probably exerted greater influence on the development of Judaism than did any other single non-Jew. It is held by some that the Book of Daniel alludes to Alexander in its reference (11:3–4) to a mighty king who will rule with great dominion and whose kingdom will be destroyed after his death. "Alexander of Macedon at the Gates of Paradise" (page 150), one of many stories of this type, is a reminder that earthly power, might, and vast possessions do not merit entry into paradise. This, of course, is a familiar theme of Jewish wit and wisdom.

The Emperor and the Deaf Man

A Christian emperor one day challenged the Jews of his capital
to a public contest in wisdom. This was to differ from all other
battles of wit between Jews and Christians: it was to be in the language of signs. On the appointed day the Jewish wise men and
scholars appeared before the emperor and his court without any
inkling of the nature of the contest. The emperor began by raising
two fingers in an aggressive gesture. He waited for a response in
sign language from his Jewish opponents, but none was forthcom-
ing. He then showed an egg to them; still no response. Finally he
took a measure of corn and scattered it on the ground. And still
the wise men of the Jews made no sign in return; unable to interpret the signs, they could not reply to them. The emperor then gave
the leaders of the community three days in which to solve the rid-
dle he had set them. If they failed at the end of the three days,
they would all be put to death.

The rabbis decreed that the three days be given up to fasting
and prayer by the entire community, and prayed for divine intervention. On the third day, a deaf man, poorly dressed, was seen
walking in the street and eating cheese. On being rebuked for his
behavior at such a time, he asked why they were fasting. When
told the reason, the deaf man showed surprise and asked to be
taken before the emperor and allowed to interpret and answer the

signs. Thereupon the leaders of the Jews took him to the imperial court.

As on the previous occasion, the emperor thrust out two fingers. Without hesitation the deaf man lifted one finger. The emperor then showed an egg. In reply the deaf man pulled out a piece of cheese from a kerchief. After that, the emperor took a measure of corn and scattered it on the ground, whereupon the deaf man gathered up the grains and wrapped them in his kerchief. So pleased with the deaf man's sagacity was the emperor that he gave him a reward and a new garment.

The Jews were overjoyed at the result and gave thanks to the Almighty for their timely deliverance from death. They were curious to know how the deaf man had been able to interpret the emperor's signs and reply in like manner. To their questions the deaf man replied: "When the emperor thrust out his two fingers he meant that he would put out my two eyes. I replied that I could do the same to him with one finger. He then showed me an egg, signifying that he had plenty of food; I, in turn, showed him my cheese, meaning that I also had ample and was in no need of anything. When he scattered the corn on the ground, I considered it a sinful act and so gathered it up."

The emperor's courtiers likewise asked their master to explain to them the hidden meaning of the signs and gestures. He answered them in the following words: "The two raised fingers referred to the belief in the duality of God: that is, God and Jesus. The Jew replied by raising one finger, meaning that his people recognize only the One God. When I showed him the egg, it was to say that Jesus was not born of man. He replied by showing the cheese, which could not be curdled without the aid of rennet, a special substance found within the stomach of an unweaned calf, and compared here to sperm; this suggests that Jesus could not have been born except as other human beings are. I scattered the corn on the ground, saying that God has scattered the Children of Israel across the face of the earth. The Jew replied, by his action, that God would gather them together again."

The Test

There was once a prince, whose wife had borne him many daughters but no son. When the princess became pregnant again, her husband said to her, "If you again bear me a daughter, I shall have you put to death."

The princess, frightened at these words, summoned the midwife and told her of the prince's threat should she bear another daughter. The midwife soothed the mother and assured her that God would protect her in the hour of her trial. When she was delivered of a child, it was found to be a daughter. Without anybody seeing her, the midwife told the princess to have no fear and took the newborn child to a place where women of the town came to draw water, leaving their babies unwatched for a short while. Seizing her chance, the midwife exchanged the girl for a boy and hurried back with him to her mistress. When the prince was told that his wife had borne a son, his joy knew no bounds; he gave a great banquet and distributed charity to the poor of the city and gave his wife precious gifts. Meanwhile, the mother of the male child discovered what had happened. Distraught, she inquired in all quarters of the city as to who had taken her newborn son and left a girl in his place. In the end the truth came out, and the two mothers were summoned before the king and his judges. The mother of the boy was asked to put her case.

"May your majesty's life be prolonged!" began the woman. "I and the princess each gave birth to a child on the same day, but I bore a boy, while she bore a girl. Since she feared her husband's wrath she found a way to rob me of my son and put her daughter in his place. When I took my child to bathe him I discovered the trick that had been played and saw that the child was a girl."

The princess denied the accusation and claimed she was the mother of the boy. The matter was put to the judges, but they were unable to pass judgment or pronounce sentence. So the king sent a high official of the court to fetch Rabbi Eliyahu, *dayyan* (judge) of the Jews and known for his wisdom and skill in judgment. When the rabbi appeared before the king, the latter acquainted him with the case and invited him to give the court his opinion. After considering the matter for a while, the *dayyan* ordered the two parties to the dispute to bring him two cups of the same size and weight. He then asked the two mothers—the princess and the second woman—to squeeze their breasts and let the milk of the one mother flow into one cup, and the milk of the other into the second. The cups were then weighed, and it was found that the woman's milk was heavier than that of the princess. Rabbi Eliyahu then gave judgment.

Turning to the wife of the prince, he said: "The other woman is the mother of the boy. Return her son to her and take back your daughter. Have no fear of your husband's anger, for I shall plead with him on your behalf."

All those assembled before the king marveled greatly at the wisdom of the *dayyan,* who showed that the milk destined to feed a boy is always heavier than the milk of the mother of a girl. The king then knew that God had indeed granted wisdom to Rabbi Eliyahu and he honored him and made him an adviser to the court.

Maimonides and the King's Dream

A certain king once dreamed a very strange dream, but, on awakening, immediately forgot what it was about. He summoned the interpreters of dreams from far and wide, but they all told him that unless he was able to tell them the contents of his dream, they could not interpret it. In the face of the king's anger and disappointment, his chief counselor promised to go out and find someone knowledgeable enough to tell the king what his dream was as well as interpret it. On his way out, the royal counselor met Moses Maimonides—who was then a boy—in the company of his teacher. The counselor thought that he would ask the teacher about somebody able to tell the king his dream, but before he could open his mouth, Maimonides broke in and informed the teacher of the counselor's errand on behalf of his master. The counselor, impressed by the boy's unusual intelligence and insight, took him before the king and told him to acquaint the monarch with the dream and its meaning.

"Your Majesty," said Maimonides, "in your dream you saw a long table on which all kinds of rich food were laid out. From a corner of the hall a swine came forth and ate of every dish on the table and then suddenly disappeared. The interpretation of the dream is this. The many dishes of food are the king's many wives, and the swine is a palace slave living with the wives."

The king then asked the young Maimonides if he was able to point out the slave. Although the latter was dressed in women's attire, Maimonides pointed him out at once. The king wanted to slay him there and then, but Maimonides advised him to carry out the deed at night without anyone's knowledge.

The Pomegranate Seed

A poor man once stole a piece of food and was ordered by the king to be hanged. On his way to the gallows, the man told one of the king's guards that he was in possession of a wonderful secret which he would like to reveal to the king; otherwise it would die with him. The guard took the man before the king, who asked him about the secret.

"I can put a pomegranate seed in the ground, and it will grow and bear fruit overnight," said the accused man. "It is a secret my father taught me, and I thought it would be a pity were it to die with me."

A time was appointed on the following day for planting the seed. The thief, the king, and his courtiers were all there. The thief then dug a hole and said: "This seed can be planted in the ground only by a man who never in his life has stolen or taken anything which did not belong to him. Being a thief, I cannot, of course, do it."

So the king turned to his vizier and ordered him to plant the seed. The vizier hesitated, then said, "Your Majesty, when I was a young man I recall keeping an article which did not belong to me. I, obviously, cannot plant this seed."

The treasurer, when told to plant the seed, begged the king's forgiveness, saying that dealing with such large sums of money as he did, he may have entered too much or too little in the records. The king, in his turn, recalled that he once took and kept a precious object belonging to his father.

The thief turned to them and said: "You are all mighty and powerful persons. You are not in want of anything, yet you cannot plant the seed; while I, who stole a little food to keep myself from starvation, am to be hanged."

The king, pleased with the man's clever ruse, laughed and pardoned him, and sent him away with a present.

The Sack of Corn

There was once a man who was wise and knowledgeable but at the same time very poor. He used to go about complaining of his lot and asking why God had dealt so harshly with him. His loud complaints eventually reached the ears of the king, who ordered the man brought before him. The king asked him why he was always bemoaning his lot. The poor man replied, "I am wise and possess much knowledge, yet I am starving. Why does God treat me in such a manner?" Taking pity on him, the king ordered a sack of corn to be delivered to him every week. Whenever the poor man received his sack of corn, he used to murmur, "It is nature."

Some time later, a merchant in precious stones offered the king a gold ring set with a precious stone which he claimed to be of one piece. The king, doubting the truth of the merchant's statement, called in the poor man to test both his wisdom and the merchant's claim. The wise man looked once at the ring and said that the precious stone was of two pieces and not one. When challenged, he put the ring in boiling water and the stone fell apart into two pieces. Thereupon the king appointed him a counselor and doubled his weekly sack of corn to two sacks. On receiving them, the poor man again said, "It is nature."

On another occasion a fine horse was presented to the king. He called in his counselor to give judgment on the horse's qualities. The man examined it and said that although it was a fine horse, its nature was vicious and that after a gallop of a certain number of miles the animal would throw its rider and kill him. In order to test the counselor's claim, a man under sentence of death was ordered to ride the horse, and after a certain distance he was thrown and killed. As a reward for his wisdom, the counselor's weekly ration of corn was increased from two to three sacks. When the sacks were delivered to him he again murmured, "It is nature."

One day a banquet was held at the palace, at which the counselor was present. During the meal he was heard to murmur, "It is nature." Someone overheard and told the king, who, after the banquet, called the counselor aside and asked him the meaning of his remark. "If my lord the king promises not to have me put to death I will reveal the secret!" he replied. The king promised and invited his counselor to speak without fear. The wise man then informed the king that his majesty was not really the son of his reputed father, but rather the son of a peasant who threshed and ground corn for a livelihood. The king went to his mother and asked if this was true. She confessed that the counselor had told the truth. The king thereupon gave the wise man great wealth and property so that he should keep the secret of the king's humble birth.

Leviathan and the Fox

The Angel of Death once demanded of God the power to slay all living things. The Almighty told him first to cast a pair of every species into the sea, and then he could have dominion over all those that remained. The Angel of Death at once cast a pair of every species into the ocean. When the fox saw what was happening, he wept bitterly.

"Why are you weeping?" asked the Angel of Death.

"For my companions whom you have cast into the sea," was the reply.

"Where are they?" inquired the angel.

In answer, the wily animal ran to the water's edge with his wife and told the Angel of Death to look down into the water. The angel did so and saw the reflection of the fox and its mate. Thinking these to be a pair of foxes already cast into the sea, he turned to the foxes still on land and said, "All right, you are free to go."

A little later the fox encountered the weasel and related how he and his wife had escaped from the clutches of the Angel of Death. The weasel went and did likewise.

At the end of a year Leviathan, king of the sea, called an assembly of all the creatures of the deep, but noticed that the fox and the weasel were not among them. Puzzled, he inquired of their whereabouts, and when he learned what had happened, he ordered a great delegation of fish to go and seek out the fox and to use cunning and guile to catch him. The fish swam off and eventually found him on the seashore. The fox greeted them politely and, in answer to their question, told them who he was.

"Indeed," exclaimed the fish, "what luck for us! You are the very person we are looking for. We have come all this way to tell you that there is a great honor in store for you. Our king, the mighty Leviathan, is very ill and at death's door. He has named you as his successor, for he has heard that you are wiser and more prudent than all other animals. Come with us and we will conduct you to him so that he may honor you before he dies."

"How can I enter the sea without being drowned?" asked the fox. "I am not like you fish whose home is in the ocean."

"Ride upon our back," answered the fish, "and we will carry you in safety above the surface of the sea. We shall then descend with you down into the deep to our kingdom without your even knowing it. Make haste and come with us, and soon you will rule the dominions of the sea. You will be safe forever from the wild beasts on land, and no longer will you be in danger of being hunted from place to place."

The fox, believing all that the fish told him, went with them into the sea, and off they started on their journey. But as soon as he felt the cold water washing around him, the fox realized that he had been tricked. "Alas!" he lamented, "what folly have I committed? I, who have played many a trick on others, have now been tricked by these fish. How shall I free myself and escape the trap they have laid?"

He thought quickly. "Look," he said, addressing the fish, "now that you have me in your power, let me speak freely with you and ask you a question. What do you want of me, and what designs have you on me?"

"We will tell you the truth," replied the fish. "Leviathan is neither ill nor dying. He has heard of your wisdom and cunning and has sworn to rend you apart and eat your heart and thus become wise and cunning like the foxes."

The fox, who had by now recovered his wits, said to the fish in a tone of surprise: "Indeed, why did you not tell me this at the beginning? I would then have brought my heart with me to present to King Leviathan and he would have honored me."

"You have not brought your heart with you?" asked the fish in astonishment. "How can that be?"

"Well, I'll tell you," said the crafty animal, "it is like this. It's the custom among us foxes to leave our hearts at home whenever we travel. If we need our heart for any purpose, then, of course, we take it with us."

"What shall we do now?" asked the bewildered fish.

"That's easy," the fox replied, "my house is just near the seashore, not far from here. If you carry me back to the place where you first saw me I will go and get my heart and return with you to your king. I shall then give my heart to Leviathan and he will reward both you and me and heap great honors on us. But if you take me into his presence without my heart, he will be angry with you and surely destroy you. It is for you fish that I fear; I do not fear on my own account. I shall say to Leviathan: 'My lord, these fish did not tell me at first what their true mission was. When they at last told me I prayed them to let me return for my heart, but they refused.'"

Impressed by this clever argument, the fish conveyed the fox back to the spot where they had first encountered him. The moment they reached the shore, the fox jumped on to dry land and began dancing with glee.

"Hurry," cried the fish, "fetch your heart and come back."

The fox laughed. "You fools," he taunted, "how could I have come with you without a heart! How can any animal live without a heart?"

"You have tricked us," wailed the fish.

"Of course I have, you simple creatures. I fooled the Angel of

Death with ease; how much more so a lot of silly fish."

And so the fish, ashamed and humiliated, returned to Leviathan and related to him what had happened. After berating them for their gullibility and stupidity, their master devoured them.

The Hypocrite and the Merchant's Pledge

One day a wealthy merchant came to the town of Sidon, in Syria, for the purpose of transacting some business. He put up at an inn but, finding himself among strangers, he feared the bag of gold he carried might be stolen. He therefore decided to seek out some trustworthy citizen in the town with whom he could leave his money while completing his business.

The next day the merchant visited a place of worship and came across an old man deep in prayer. From the demeanor of the worshipper and his fervent and devout praying to his Creator, the visitor felt certain that here was a pious and Godfearing person whom he could trust with his wealth. After the service was over, the merchant went up to greet the old man and introduced himself.

"I am a merchant and a stranger in your city," he said, "and I'm looking for an honest and upright man with whom I can entrust my wealth while I transact my business here. Having seen you at prayer with such devotion and fervor, I feel you are a trustworthy person with whom I can leave my money for safekeeping. Will you do me this favor and look after it for me?"

The old man agreed to do what the merchant asked and took the bag of gold, promising solemnly that he would keep it in safety. Some time later, the merchant, having completed his business, went to the old man's house to claim his pledge and redeem his money. But the old man pretended not to know his visitor and denied having received any gold from him for safekeeping.

"I don't know what you're talking about," he shouted. "I've never set eyes on you before in my life." The more the stranger insisted he had left the bag of gold with the old man, the more the latter abused him for being a liar and a trickster. He drove him from his door.

Greatly troubled, the merchant went again to the old man's house, but was met with curses and insults. In despair he sought the advise of a business acquaintance, a shrewd merchant from Tarshish, and asked him how he could recover his pledge from the old rascal.

"Do not worry, my brother," replied the man from Tarshish. "I shall see that justice is done, and I shall compel this hypocrite to return your money to you. Tomorrow you shall see what I will do."

The following day the Tarshish merchant took a bag of gold and silver and said to his friend: "I am now going to the house of the old man to try and get back your property. I shall have to use craft and cunning to induce him to return the gold. Now, at a certain hour—when I will be present there—go to his house and claim the money you left with him."

The wise merchant of Tarshish then went to the old man's house. The latter opened the door to him and greeted him extravagantly, asking what service he could do for the stranger who had honored him. The visitor returned the greeting in like manner, and said:

"I am a merchant from Tarshish and am here to transact some urgent business, but I have a daughter living in a distant town whom I wish to see. Now, I have in my possession a large sum of money and many valuables, and I fear to take them with me on my journey, lest I be robbed by brigands. Having heard from many people that you are an upright and Godfearing man, I have decided to leave my money and valuables in your care for safekeeping until my return. I know I can trust you, for everybody I have met praises your honesty and good faith."

"Well have you spoken," said the old man. "Leave your money and your valuables with me and visit your daughter with an easy mind. On the day of your return to Sidon I will hand you back all your property."

"And now I request you," said the merchant, "to write my name and that of my father on my bag, since there are many impostors and deceivers about, and one of them might come and claim my property as his own."

While this was being done, the first merchant suddenly appeared, in accordance with the arrangement, and, greeting the old man with respect, said:

"Honored master, I have now completed all my business in this town and am about to depart. Before doing so, however, I would like to receive back the bag of gold I deposited with you on my arrival."

The old man saw that there was nothing to do but hand back the money to its rightful owner. He turned to him, saying,

"My sight is weak; come over here, my friend, that I may touch you and be assured that you are indeed the man who entrusted his money to me." Fearing that the man of Tarshish would change his mind and refuse to leave his wealth and valuables in his keeping, the old man spoke again to the first merchant:

"You are indeed the man who deposited with me a bag of gold for safekeeping. A short while ago an impostor strangely resembling you came to me and laid claim to your money, but I spoke harsh words to him and drove him from my house. Now, however, I am certain that you are the rightful owner of this money, and I return to you your property."

Thereupon the old man handed back the bag of gold, and the merchant took it and departed.

Alexander of Macedon at the Gates of Paradise

Among the many stories told about Alexander the Great is an account of how he reached the gates of paradise while still on earth. One day, having conquered all the known world, the Macedonian came upon a small river flowing between peaceful banks fragrant with the perfume of many flowers. He was puzzled, for he did not know this river, so he resolved to follow its course to see where it would lead. He marched for many days along its banks till he finally arrived at the gates of paradise. Finding the gates locked against him, he hammered on them and demanded to be admitted.

"Who's there?" a voice called from the garden.

"It is I, Alexander the Macedonian, conqueror of the world, master of the universe, and mighty ruler. Open the gates of paradise that I may enter."

The voice replied: "Who is Alexander? This is the abode of the righteous, the city of peace. Only the just and those who have conquered their passions may pass through these gates. The powerful and the mighty and the rulers over vast dominions have no place here. Nations have bowed down before you and paid tribute and homage to you, but your soul is not worthy of admittance to the city of the just. Go back; heal your soul and gather wisdom."

The world-conqueror pleaded with the guardian of the gate to let him enter, but his entreaties were of no avail. At last, Alexander, in despair, asked the guardian of paradise to give him something that he might show to people as testimony and proof that he had reached the gates of paradise, and stood where no mortal had ever stood before. The guardian of the city of the blessed relented and threw Alexander the fragment of a human skull, saying: "Take this and weigh it against gold."

Alexander called for a pair of scales, and placed the piece of bone on one and a quantity of gold on the other. To his great astonishment the fragment of skull outweighed the gold. More gold was added, then more, but no matter how much of the precious metal was heaped up against it, the bone still outweighed it. The Macedonian marveled at this but could not understand it. "Is there anything that will outweigh this fragment of a human skull?" he asked.

For an answer, a wise man who was present there removed the pile of gold and threw in its place a handful of dust from the ground. At once the scale holding the piece of skull shot upwards as the handful of earth outweighed it.

A King and Destiny

Next to the palace of a certain king stood a tumble-down hut where a poor and unfortunate man lived. The king wanted to find some way of destroying his neighbor's mean dwelling without incurring the wrath of the people.

One day one of the royal advisers suggested to his master that he offer a large sum of money to his poverty-stricken neighbor in the hope of inducing him to demolish his hut and put up in its place a fine new house, and thus avoid offense to his kingly neighbor. The king agreed to this suggestion and, calling his neighbor to the palace, said to him: "Spread your cloak upon the ground." The poor man did as he was bidden and spread his cloak upon the ground, whereupon the king ordered it to be filled with gold and silver coins. The man then gathered up his cloak, tied the ends together, making it into a sack to carry the money, and made his way back to his hovel. In the street he passed two men fighting. He stopped to see what the quarrel was about but got too close to the disputants, with the result that the cloak containing the money was inadvertently knocked out of his hands and the gold and silver coins were scattered all over the roadway. In no time passersby had snatched up every coin in sight, leaving the unlucky owner with just one silver piece. He gathered up his cloak and returned to his hut with bitterness and rage at his bad luck.

A few days later the king again called the poor man to the palace. "What did you do with the money I gave you?" he asked. His neighbor sighed and told the king what had happened. "Never mind," was the king's response, "you are not to blame for what has happened. I will give you more money—much more than I gave you last time."

The poor man took the money and blessed the king for his generosity. No sooner did he set off than he slipped on a piece of melon rind and fell, and his money, as before, was scattered all over the road. Again the crowds snatched up the money, leaving the man with only his cloak. A few days later the king called him to the palace, and when he heard what had happened he grew angry and scolded and upbraided the poor man.

"It's not my fault," protested the unfortunate man. "It's the fault of my black luck. Nothing can prevail against it, and there is nothing one can do."

"That's not true!" shouted the king, and he drove the wretch from his presence. The latter returned home in misery and humiliation.

But, in spite of his anger, the king did not despair. He decided to let his poor neighbor have more money; but this time he sent it through an emissary to make quite certain that it would arrive safely and not be lost on the way. The next day the king went in disguise to find out what his neighbor was doing with the large sum of money that had been sent him the day before. On arrival at the entrance to the poor man's dwelling, the king found him lying on the ground, lifeless. On the man's forehead was written in letters of fire these words: "O king, I made him poor; and you enriched him. I have now killed him; you now try and bring him back to life."

Only then did the king understand that one cannot fly in the face of destiny.

The Golem

Introduction

The word *golem* in early and medieval Hebrew had the meaning "embryo," "shapeless mass," "formless matter." It later came to signify the clay model of a man created by human hands for specific purposes. In popular Jewish legend, a special ritual was employed to infuse life into it: a tablet inscribed with one of the Holy Names of God was placed beneath the golem's tongue or on its forehead. The golem would then obey automatically the commands of its master. It did not have the power of either speech or reason.

A number of medieval Jewish figures are credited with having created golems. But by far the best known is that of the celebrated thinker, scholar, and mystic, the great Rabbi Judah Löw (or Liwa) ben Bezalel of Prague (1512–1609). Known as the Maharal, from the Hebrew initials of his name, Rabbi Löw created the Golem, whom he called Joseph, for the specific purpose of frustrating the evil plots against the Jewish people. How the miracle-working rabbi created the Golem with the assistance of two disciples (one his son-in-law) is described in full in "The Golem of Rabbi Judah Löw" (page 159 ff.). We learn from this and the following stories that Joseph the Golem ran errands and did many other odd jobs in the rabbi's school.

When the prime reason for the Golem's existence ceased because of the changed circumstances of the Jewish community, its creator, the Maharal, decided that the time had come for it to be destroyed. In "The End of the Golem" (page 169 ff.), we see how its destruction was achieved.

Many legends grew up around the Maharal in the eighteenth century, and it was during that period that the many tales of the golem became associated with his personality. Much of the legendary material is said to have been written down by Rabbi Löw's son-in-law, Rabbi Yizhaq Kohen, and preserved in manuscript for three hundred years. One authority on Rabbi Löw, Frederic Thierberger, however, in *The Great Rabbi Löw of Prague,* casts doubt on the historical authenticity of that document. For while the work shows knowledge of the Maharal's family affairs, it displays ignorance of the position of the Jews of Prague at that time. The emperor said to have issued the edict to the effect that the charges against the Jews were false is Rudolf II; but during his rule the position of the Jews was favorable and no accusation of so-called ritual murder was brought against them.

Whatever the facts of history may be, in the popular mind Rabbi Judah Löw, as the eminent teacher and spiritual leader of Prague Jewry, will always be best known as the creator of the golem, a major figure in Jewish legend.

The Golem of Rabbi Judah Löw

Rabbi Judah Löw, son of Bezalel, was the celebrated rabbi of Prague and the *Ab Bet Din* * of that city's Jewish community. A great scholar, he was well versed in holy law and known for his learning in rabbinical literature and mysticism; he was also knowledgeable in a number of foreign tongues. During Rabbi Judah's time, the Jews of Prague suffered a number of discriminations and were falsely accused of practicing so-called "ritual murder." The pious son of Bezalel was much exercised by this and often prayed for divine guidance to enable him to ameliorate the lot of his people and refute the slanderous charges made against them by the local clergy.

One night Rabbi Judah Löw had a vision in which he heard a voice tell him to fashion a human image of clay and by this means help frustrate the evil plots against his flock. In the morning he summoned both his son-in-law and his favorite disciple and acquainted them with the command he had received. He also sought their help in the great task he was about to undertake. "Four elements are required," he said, "for the creation of the Golem: earth, water, fire, and air. I possess the power of the wind, my son-in-law stands for fire, and my favorite pupil is the symbol of

* Head of the Jewish court of justice.

water. Thus the three of us together will be able to undertake this work." The rabbi bound his two companions to secrecy and asked them to set aside seven days in order to prepare for their task.

By the end of the week the three men were ready. Four hours after midnight they made their way to the banks of a river on the outskirts of the city, where they found a loam pit. From the malleable clay—the element earth—they made the figure of a man three ells in height. They then fashioned the features and the feet and laid the clay figure on its back on the ground. The first part of their task completed, the three men stood at the feet of the image. Then Rabbi Judah commanded his son-in-law to circle it seven times while reciting a Kabbalistic formula which he, the rabbi, had composed. As soon as the son-in-law had completed the seventh circle and recited the formula in accordance with his father-in-law's instructions, the clay figure began to glow like a live coal; then the holy man commanded his disciple to do likewise, that is, walk round the image seven times while reciting another formula. On completion of the disciple's circling, the heat of the figure diminished. The image began to grow moist, and vapor arose from it. At the same time nails appeared on the tips of its fingers and toes, and hair on its head. The face of the clay image was that of a man about thirty years of age. Finally, Rabbi Judah himself circled the figure seven times, and the three learned men recited the following verse: "And the Lord God formed man of the dust of the ground and breathed into his nostrils the breath of life; and the man became a living soul" (Genesis 2:7).

On the reciting of this passage from holy writ the Golem's eyes opened and looked with wonder and awe upon the rabbi and his two disciples. The master then commanded the Golem to arise from the ground. The man of clay immediately stood upright. The three then clothed the Golem with garments and shoes they had brought, the clothes worn by the beadle of the synagogue. The rabbi then spoke the following words to the image that he and his companions had created:

"Know, O clod of earth, that we have fashioned you from dust in order that you may protect the people of Israel from their adversaries and guard them against calumny and slander, suffering and distress. Your name shall henceforth be Joseph, and you will dwell in the *Bet Din* * over which I preside, and you shall do the work of a servant. You shall obey all my commands and do what I bid you, and go through fire and through water and throw yourself from a high tower." The Golem inclined its head as if to acknowledge the rabbi's words. It comported itself in every way like a human being. Although it lacked the power of speech, it could hear and understand all that was said. The night's labor completed, the three men returned to the rabbi's house, taking the Golem with them.

Rabbi Judah Löw kept the strange ceremony secret; and in order to explain the presence of the Golem he told his household that as he had been returning from the ritual bath early in the morning he had met a beggar and brought him home to work as a servant in the schoolroom where his pupils studied. But he forbade any member of his family to make the stranger do domestic work about the house. From that time on, the Golem sat in a corner of the schoolroom, its head in its hands. It sat motionless in that manner except when its pious master commanded it to perform some task. Neither fire nor water could harm the Golem, nor could any sword wound it. The rabbi had called his creation Joseph after the Joseph Shida mentioned in the Talmud, of whom it is related that he was half human and half demon and had performed many services for the Rabbis.

According to tradition, the miracle-working rabbi had created the Golem for the sole purpose of helping defend the Jews of Prague against blood accusations. The only work permitted it involved certain tasks about the school.

The way in which the Golem was employed to do the task for which it was created was as follows. The master had the power to render the Golem invisible by hanging around its neck a talisman in the form of an amulet inscribed on the skin of a hart. During

* Court of justice.

the week preceding Passover, the Golem was instructed to walk through the streets of Prague and stop any person who was carrying a heavy sack on his back to see what it contained because such sacks sometimes contained a dead body which the carrier intended to dump in the Jewish quarter of the town so that its inhabitants could be charged with murder. If the sack contained a body, the Golem immediately tied up the man with a piece of rope and delivered him up to the authorities for punishment. In such fashion did the Golem carry out the duties imposed upon it by its master.

The Golem and the Bridal Pair

When Rabbi Judah was *Ab Bet Din* of Prague, two well-to-do merchants, who were also business partners, built a spacious house which they and their families jointly inhabited. The wife of one of the merchants had borne strong, healthy children, while the other's wife had given birth to weak and sickly children, some of whom died. The latter woman was jealous of the other and envied her robust offspring. She took care, however, not to let her feelings betray her, and harbored her pain within her breast. The midwife who had attended the two women at childbirth knew the truth and vowed to herself that one day she would help the unhappy woman.

Her opportunity came one day when the two wives gave birth to male children within the same hour. The midwife observed that the child of the one woman was stronger and larger than that of the other. Fearing that the weak child might die, she decided to exchange the children and substitute one for the other. She carried out her plan at night, when both families were asleep. In consequence, each mother suckled the baby she imagined to be her own offspring, not realizing that she was suckling the other woman's child. The two boys grew up; no one suspected that those whom they respectively knew as their father and mother were not their real parents. In time, the midwife died and took her secret with her to the grave.

When the boys reached manhood, the father of the robust children decided it was time that his youngest son—in reality his neighbor's son—married. He chose for the boy's bride the daughter of his business partner. This was agreed to by the parents, and a deed of betrothal was drawn up. The day of marriage arrived. Rabbi Judah, who had been invited to conduct the wedding ceremony and bless the union, in accordance with custom took a glass of wine in his hand and was about to pronounce the benediction. The glass dropped from his hand and fell shattered to the ground. The rabbi took another cup of wine and this, too, fell broken to the ground. All present at the ceremony were seized with fright, and Rabbi Judah turned pale and trembled. Such a strange happening seemed to portend evil.

Rabbi Judah thereupon summoned Joseph, the Golem, and ordered him to fetch more wine at once. Joseph ran quickly to the master's wine-cellar. As he hurried across the room, the wedding guests noticed him nodding his head and making signs to some invisible person. When he reached the cellar, Joseph stopped and, instead of entering to get more wine, went toward Rabbi Judah's courtroom. There he hastily scribbled a few words on a piece of paper and handed it to his master. Reading it, the good rabbi was seized with trembling and fear. On the paper handed him was written: "The bridegroom and bride are brother and sister."

Joseph then made signs to the master as if to communicate something else. Rabbi Judah turned to the assembled guests and told them that the wedding ceremony would not be performed that day. After that he left the synagogue, accompanied by the Golem. Outside the building they encountered the spirit that had revealed to Joseph the secret concerning the bridal pair.

Rabbi Judah was determined to get to the bottom of the matter and solve the mystery. Early the following day, before morning prayers, the miracle-working rabbi ordered a wooden partition to be erected in a corner of the synagogue hall. When the worshipers arrived for morning service, Rabbi Judah asked them to stay behind after prayers. The service over, he and his two assistant judges, still wearing their prayer-shawls, seated themselves at a table. The beadle was sent to bring the bridal pair and their respective parents to the synagogue. When they arrived, Rabbi Löw commanded the Golem, in the hearing of the entire congregation, to go to the cemetery and summon the dead midwife. He gave Joseph a staff with which to knock on the woman's tomb and waken her from her sleep. The assembled people were dumb with terror, but the rabbi calmed them with soothing words.

"Have no fear," he said, "be assured that no harm will befall you."

After a while, Joseph reappeared and, handing the staff back to the master, gestured toward the wooden partition as if to indicate that he had carried out the rabbi's command and had led the spirit of the dead woman there. Again a terrible fear gripped those present, and all sat rigid as if petrified. Then suddenly they heard Rabbi Judah call out in a loud clear voice:

"We, the earthly court of justice, command you to speak and tell us the truth concerning the bride and bridegroom and how it happens they are sister and brother."

The soul of the departed midwife then began to relate all that had taken place when the two children were born. The congregation could hear the voice from behind the screen, but only the judges, the bridal pair, and the two sets of parents were able to distinguish the words. The dead woman confessed that during the many years that had elapsed since her departure from this world, her soul had found no rest because of what she had done. It was only on account of the great piety of Rabbi Judah that she had been permitted to stop the wedding and thus repair the wrong she had committed. Having thus spoken, the dead woman burst out into loud lamentations, and those present wept with her.

Rabbi Judah then took counsel with his fellow judges concerning the sentence they should pronounce. It was finally decreed that the dead midwife should ask forgiveness of the couple and their parents. Weeping loudly, the spirit of the deceased woman obeyed, and she was then allowed to depart in peace. Since the affianced couple were in reality brother and sister, they were forbidden to marry each other. And so through this miraculous intervention a sinful union was prevented.

Why the Scroll of the Law Fell to the Ground

Joseph the Golem proved to be of service to his master and the community in several ways; and he was able to help Rabbi Judah in connection with a distressing incident that happened on the Day of Atonement in the Great Synagogue of Prague.

During the afternoon service, one of the worshipers who had been called up to raise aloft the Scroll of the Law after the reading of the prescribed portion let it fall from his hands. The Maharal was greatly distressed, for a sin had been committed which would have to be expiated. He proclaimed at once that all present should fast for a whole day before the advent of Sukkot (Feast of Tabernacles). But the rabbi continued to be very exercised over the episode. The more he thought about it, the clearer it became to him that such things do not usually come to pass without good and sufficient cause. He decided to find out more.

On the day of the fast Rabbi Löw prayed fervently that he be vouchsafed the answer in a dream. His prayer was answered, and that night he dreamed that he heard a jumble of words whose sense he could not grasp. On awakening he remembered the words and found that they consisted of fifteen letters in all. He wrote down each one on a separate piece of paper and then called Joseph and commanded him to shuffle the slips of paper and arrange them on the table.

Joseph did as his master ordered, placing the fifteen slips of paper next to one another without paying much attention to what was written on them. But the letters so arranged formed no known words. After studying the papers for a while, the rabbi saw that they formed the initial letters of a verse from the Bible which was part of the Torah reading for the Day of Atonement. It referred to the sanctity of married life and the sin of adultery.

The Maharal then called before him the man who had dropped the Torah Scroll and demanded that he confess that he had had intercourse with another man's wife. His sinful action had been responsible for the happening on the Day of Atonement. The man saw that it would be useless to deny his guilt, so he confessed and suffered the penance imposed on him. And in accordance with the law, the woman who had lain with him was likewise punished.

The End of the Golem

An edict was finally issued by the emperor to the effect that the so-called blood accusation was false and without foundation. Henceforth all further charges against the Jews of Prague in that connection were forbidden by the authorities.

In view of this new law, Rabbi Judah Löw now decided that the time had come to destroy the Golem, since the prime reason for its existence had ceased to exist. Having made this decision, the Maharal informed his two pupils of his intent. He then ordered the Golem not to sleep in the courtroom that night but to make its bed in the loft of the Great Synagogue. This the Golem did.

About two o'clock in the morning the rabbi and his two pupils went up to the loft and stood by the bed of the sleeping Golem. Rabbi Judah then commanded the two men to walk round the Golem seven times, but in reverse order. When the seventh circuit had been completed, the Golem returned to its original state—a lifeless piece of clay. The Maharal then divested it of its garments and wrapped it in two old prayer-shawls. After this the three men took the heavy mass of earth and hid it out of sight among the many old books lying in the loft. The clothes and the bed were later burned secretly.

On the following day the news spread around the town that the

Golem had disappeared, and it was assumed that Joseph had run away. Two weeks later, Rabbi Löw issued an order that on no account was any person to go up to the synagogue loft. It was generally assumed that the rabbi's order was a precaution against the risk of fire. Only a handful of people knew the real reason.

Many stories, it is said, were related by the Maharal in connection with his creation of the Golem. One is that when he was about to breathe the breath of life into the clay figure, two spirits had manifested themselves to the master: those of the demons Joseph and Jonathan, both called Shida. He chose the name of the former, since this Joseph had performed many services for the Talmudic rabbis. The Maharal's Golem had many limitations: it had no power of speech; it was, of course, soulless; and it was possessed of only limited powers of discernment. Higher wisdom and real intelligence were beyond its reach. It was said that on the Sabbath day, though the Golem was not possessed of a soul, there was something different in its bearing and appearance: its face looked more impressive than it did on weekdays, and more friendly.

It is also related that every Friday, just before evening, Rabbi Löw was in the habit of removing the tablet on which he had inscribed the Ineffable Name from under the Golem's tongue, since he feared last the Sabbath render the Golem immortal and men be induced to worship it as a god. The Golem was neither good nor bad; whatever action it did was under compulsion. Some say that it obeyed out of fear that it might be turned back into dust. Once the Golem had been given instructions by its master and charged with the carrying out of any task determined by him, nothing could prevent it.